Jeanne Stevens

SOUL SCHOOL

Enrolling in a Soulful Lifestyle
for Youth Ministry

FOREWORD BY DOUG FIELDS

ZONDERVAN.com/
AUTHORTRACKER
follow your favorite authors

youth
specialties

youth specialties

Soul School: Enrolling in a Soulful Lifestyle for Youth Ministry
Copyright © 2007 by Jeanne Stevens

Youth Specialties products, 300 South Pierce Street, El Cajon, CA 92020 are published by Zondervan, 5300 Patterson Ave. SE, Grand Rapids, MI 49530.

Library of Congress Cataloging-in-Publication Data

Stevens, Jeanne.
  Soul school : enrolling in a soulful lifestyle for youth ministry / by Jeanne Stevens.
    p. cm.
  ISBN-10: 0-310-27496-6 (pbk.)
  ISBN-13: 978-0-310-27496-4 (pbk.)
  1. Church youth workers—Religious life. 2. Church work with youth. I. Title.
  BV4596.Y68S74 2007
  259'.23—dc22

2007017349

Interior design by Mark Novelli, IMAGO MEDIA

Printed in the United States

---

07 08 09 10 11 12 13 14 15 16 17 18 • *18 17 16 15 14 13 12 11 10 9 8 7 6 5 4 3 2 1*

To Dad:

There is no one who would be more amazed

and proud that I actually wrote a book.

Your life and memory continue to remind me to

live every moment to the fullest.

SOUL SCHOOL SYLLABUS

Acknowledgments

I never imagined my soul journey would end up in a book. I'm still shocked that it has all come together. There are so many people who have been used by God to help shape me along the way. No soulish adventure should be done in isolation, and I am grateful for the role each of you has played along the way.

Sheryl Fleisher: Thank you for introducing me to my true self. I am more of who God created me to be because of you. *My Wise Women—Nancy Ortberg, Nancy Beach, & Sibyl Towner:* Thanks for speaking truth, offering grace, and believing in me along the way. *BABS—April, Becca, & Kelly:* Thanks for being real and raw. You are TRUE friends. *Ami:* I am grateful that even though we live thousands of miles apart we still have managed to travel through life together. *My Friends (you know who you are):* Thanks for reminding me when I wanted to give up that *Soul School* needed to be written. *Craig Joseph:* Thank you for pushing me to write what I really believe. Your input on this project was invaluable to me.

Willow Creek Community Church: I will be forever grateful to the community of people with whom I've shared life at Willow. You became home to me, and I am humbled to have been part of such an amazing church for the past 11 years. *The Student Ministry Staff, Volunteers, & Students I've served over the years:* Thank you for allowing me to be a part of the adventure. *Bo Boshers:* Thanks for believing in me when I was just 22 years old. Your love and leadership have deeply impacted my life. *Bill Hybels:* Thanks for speaking the truth and encouraging me to enroll in the graduate school of character. This book is the result of your prompting.

The Youth Specialties Family: I am honored to be part of an organization that takes such risks to love youth workers. *Jay Howver:* Thanks for your patience and for believing I have something to say. *Marko Oestricher:* Thanks for being my junior high youth pastor. I still can't believe how our story has been written. I love working with you. *Tic Long:* You are one of the best listeners. To follow in your footsteps is a humbling honor. *Zondervan, specifically John Raymond:* You saw potential in me as a writer before I believed it was possible. I look forward to the adventure ahead. *Doug Davidson:* I loved working with you on this project. You are so much more than an editor. You helped me find language for what was living within my soul. *Doug Fields:* Thanks for how you have encouraged and inspired countless youth workers throughout the years, including me. Your example and perseverance have reminded me that being a youth worker is a sacred calling! I am honored that you would write the foreword to this book. *Mark Novelli:* I am grateful that you have artfully designed what we were able to experience together in ministry.

Mom: I am so grateful that of all the women on the planet God picked you to be my mom. You are kind, compassionate, generous, and courageous. I admire your faith and strength. *My family (Pieczynskis & Stevens)*: Thanks for your encouragement and support.

Elijah: You are the joy of my life. This book was birthed during the first year of your life. You have no idea how you've caused me to grow. Your very existence has pushed me to travel to deeper places of faith, hope, and love. I love being your Mommy!

Jarrett: Words cannot express my love and devotion to you. You are real, honest, kind, strong, and compassionate. You are the single greatest force God has used to shape my soul. Your love and encouragement kept me going when I wanted to give up. You have stood with me during light and dark. I love you.

Foreword

By Doug Fields

When I began working in youth ministry as a volunteer in 1979, I thought it was about playing games and having fun—and that when it was time to "get serious," the job of the adult leaders was to direct teenagers' hearts to connect with the heart of God. I had no idea that so much of youth ministry would revolve around the condition of my heart, and that I would regularly have to give consideration to the depth or shallowness of my own soul.

I wish I could have read Soul School back then...it would have saved me some pain and helped me establish healthy priorities that took me too many years to figure out. As a veteran youth worker, I now know that what Jeanne writes in Soul School is right on target and essential for today's youth ministry leader (actually, any ministry leader). Joining Jeanne in Soul School won't be easy...but it will be good! It is an essential education you'll need if you're going to remain a healthy, vibrant, and effective youth ministry leader. Your teenagers need you to enroll in Soul School. (Just be thankful it won't take you four years to read this book!)

You might think it would be relatively easy to consider and reflect on the condition of your soul. After all, your soul's contents shouldn't be surprising--you've either been neglecting or reflecting on them for your entire life. But, like school, soul work requires commitment, consistency, passion, and evaluation. Since those actions aren't easy, many ministry leaders consciously or subconsciously allow their souls to run on "auto pilot" and rarely, if ever, give them the attention needed. Thankfully, the youth ministry world now has Jeanne's book as a tool to make soul work a little easier.

I'm convinced many youth ministries around the world would be healthier if we leaders got in the regular habit of assessing the state of our souls. If we did this, we might be able to prevent the damage that's been inflicted on our souls from spreading into healthy parts of our lives, causing moral, emotional, and spiritual breakdowns.

My guess is that you're holding this book because you want to be different. You want to be unique. You want to be effective. You want your soul to be healthy. That's great! This book will help you...no, really...it will help you. It's what you need, what your soul is longing for. Facing your own soul condition can be intimidating without the proper guidance—and thankfully, Jeanne's words are wise, encouraging, and experienced.

I've had the privilege to be with Jeanne a few times around the world (literally—in America and Germany) and I really like what I see! Sure, I'm impressed by her incredible ministry skills, her experience, and her strong teaching gifts—even from a distance it's obvious she's a model youth worker. But more important to me is what I see up close when I'm around her. I'm so impressed with the condition of her own soul, her love for Jesus, her passion for teenagers, and her compassion for youth ministry peers like you and me. I felt known, loved, and cared for as I read Jeanne's book. She doesn't write from an ivory tower of soul theory—she's done her own hard work and reflection and writes in such a transparent way that it's obvious she understands my fears, hurts, and the realities of fast-paced ministry. As Jeanne shares the struggles of her own ministry and personal life, I promise you'll be encouraged. You won't feel alone in your journey. Actually, I thought I was really messed up until I read Jeanne's stories (just kidding)! But I love that she's experienced some failure and is willing to share it and encourage us along the way. (You're the real deal, Jeanne, and I'm proud to be a coworker in youth ministry with you).

I wasn't really ready to go back to school, but I'm joining Jeanne in Soul School for the rest of my life! There's so much more to learn! Let's get started, the bell is about to ring and class will soon be in session...

A fellow student,
Doug Fields
Saddleback Church

Welcome to Soul School!

COURSE DESCRIPTION

I've always loved the first day of school. As a child I'm sure my excitement about going back to school had nothing to do with learning—it was all the other perks that went with it. My parents used to get me a back-to-school outfit that always included a new pair of shoes and a backpack. I loved the feeling of having fresh school supplies: sharp pencils, stiff notebooks filled with blank paper, and a brand new box of crayons ready for creating. I loved finding out who was in my class each year and picking a seat in the classroom on the first day. I loved seeing the friends I didn't get to hang out with throughout the summer, and I loved meeting my new teacher. I never dreaded going back to school in the fall because of the bow of excitement and new beginnings I tied around the package of learning.

Even as I grew and school became more demanding and less glamorous, my excitement over the first day of class never changed. Maybe it was the clean slate that each new semester provided, but I always felt energized as my professor handed out a syllabus detailing all I would learn, experience, and be required to accomplish. If only the optimism I experienced on the first day of classes each year could have stayed with me when I was cramming for a midterm halfway through the semester, or when I was up at 3:00 a.m. before the last day of class, trying to write a final paper that seemed to make no sense. The starry-eyed excitement I felt at the beginning of each school year always faded when the hard work of learning entered the equation.

My experience in student ministry has been similar to my educational journey. When I began my professional ministry adventure as a young, vibrant, vision-filled youth worker, I had high hopes about what ministry would be like. I was convinced I was entering a sacred calling that would make every workday feel like a mountaintop high. I could hardly believe I'd be getting a paycheck to do the things I loved most. On that first day, if I'd been given a real syllabus detailing just how hard ministry can be, I'm not sure I would have believed it. But the mid-semester valley of disenchantment, loneliness, insecurity, and pain came early on in my ministry run. Today, I am grateful for what I experienced in that first valley—and the others that would follow—because those difficult times were what led me to enroll in Soul School. And it's been the time

I've spent in God's School of the Soul that has given me the steadfast commitment to endure and stay in the course.

I've spent the past ten years at the same church, working in what we call the Next Generation Department. Over this decade of service, I've watched a lot of youth leaders come and go. When they arrive, they are excited, energized, and passionate. On the surface they appear to be fairly healthy and ready to run. But I've watched too many of them leave with an overwhelming sense of how exhausted they are. It's not just their eyes and their bodies, but their souls. It's as if the caffeine they were injecting into the most crucial parts of their operating systems—their souls—just couldn't keep them ticking anymore. Each time I've watched another gifted leader walk away from this sacred calling, my heart has felt a deeper burden to help the youth ministers God has called to work with this generation. I long to help these youth leaders keep their souls alive and their ministry shoes laced. I want to see their passions increase, to watch them continue to discover themselves and embrace the unique contributions they have to offer the church.

Soul School was written out of my own experience in student ministry—and my experience of watching and accompanying many others as they walked the same journey. My hope and prayer is that it will enrich and embolden your life and, ultimately, your ministry. But *Soul School* is very different from most other youth ministry books. It's not a nifty little manual with a few helpful steps to freedom. It's not a quick-read, feel-good, put-on-your-shelf-when-you're-done kind of book. You won't find any secrets to help you plan events that attract more students or mobilize more volunteers for your ministry.

Soul School is designed to take you on a journey into the deeper parts of your heart and soul. It is for any youth minister—from fresh rookie to seasoned veteran—who seeks to develop a better understanding of who he or she is. This book is about hope. It is about enrolling in the greatest adventure of discovery—the discovery of the true God and a true self.

I pray that this book will open doors in your life that may have been shut for quite some time. I pray that it will help you ask questions that will begin to illuminate the "whys" behind the frivolous, busy activity that characterizes the lives of most youth workers. I pray it will give names to the destructive patterns in your life and give you a blueprint for building emotional health and strength of the soul.

I pray this book will lead you to enroll in a lifetime in God's School of the Soul.

Welcome to class!

COURSE OBJECTIVES

The objective of *Soul School* is to point readers toward a lifetime commitment of learning to live, love, and lead from the soul. It is intended as a doorway to an ongoing course of study that any youth worker can enroll in at any point on their ministry pilgrimage.

Soul School is a different kind of class. Along the way, there will be different assignments, tests, labs, and maybe even a pop quiz or two, but there's no final exam that determines a grade for the course. This book should be read with a pen and a journal. Its pages should be marked, underlined, questioned, and discussed. There may be moments when you need to pause and stop reading for a while so you can give your soul the space that it needs to process. I encourage you to take the time you need.

Soul School is an invitation of discovery; it is not a 3-credit class to rush through and check off your list of required courses. The best way to read this book is with a personal commitment to authentic growth and soul awakening. If you're ready to enroll you can use the commitment statement below to make a covenant with God and yourself that you are willing to do the challenging but beneficial work of learning to live from your soul.

SOUL SCHOOL COMMITMENT STATEMENT

I commit myself today to enroll in the School of the Soul. I am open and ready to engage with the content of the course. I will wrestle with the internal questions that come up for me as part of this journey. I will place myself in a posture of humility and attentiveness to the Holy Spirit's voice. I will do my best to be honest with myself and with God. I will continue as a student in this School of the Soul so I can learn to live, love, and lead from this place of the soul—and help others to do so.

_____   _____   (sign your name)
             (date)

SECTION ONE

Looking Up

It was a hot summer day in the Midwest: July 9, 1999, to be specific. The air was humid, but with a slight breeze. The flowers were in full bloom. Creation was as alive as it could be. The whole earth seemed to be celebrating.

But I could not celebrate with it. In my life, it was the dead of winter. My heart felt cold. I wanted to be alone and hibernate. After some very painful experiences in the high school ministry I was helping to lead, I was now without a job. Furthermore, I felt like I had no purpose.

I began looking through a book a friend had given me called *When the Heart Waits*. Today that book sits at the top of my recommended reading list, and my original copy has more sentences underlined than not. But at that time, I'd never heard of the book or its author, Sue Monk Kidd. Yet as I paged through the book, I felt as if she'd written it just for me. I was especially drawn to a passage in her chapter "Letting Go" that seemed to bring to light the journey I was now beginning. God wanted to recover his rightful role in my life. He was inviting me to dance again as his daughter, friend, follower, and minister. But the journey would require a crucifixion, a long wait in a tomb, and a resurrection—in God's timing, not my own.

Here's what Sue Monk Kidd has to say about the challenge of letting go:

> We have a deep longing to grow and become a new creature, but we possess an equally strong compulsion to remain the same—to burrow down in our safe, secure places. The truth is that we are a patchwork of light and dark, torn between what Quaker writer Thomas Kelly called "The enhancement of our own little selves and the God possessed will." Shifting from a self-centered focus to a more God-centered focus is terribly hard. I think we've gone wrong in assuming that such a radical movement can be achieved simply by setting our jaw and saying one or two prayers of relinquishment. Letting go isn't one step but many. It's a winding, spiraling process that happens on deep levels. And we must begin at the beginning: by confronting our ambivalence."

Could it be that I was ambivalent to God? Maybe, or maybe not...but my soul was paying attention. For the first time I was really, really, really willing to go on the journey. I was willing to dive beneath the surface, to bathe in the freeing river of grace, and to look at the false idols in my life. I was open. I was hungry. I was ready to have God truly be God in my life—ready to release control, to sit back, to be confronted, and to wait.

This first section of *Soul School* is certainly not the final word on how to recalibrate oneself spiritually. But in it, I share pieces of my own journey and some of the things I learned along the way. I'm thankful that God has graciously allowed me to work through these struggles while continuing to minister to students. My lessons in the School of the Soul have often been learned in the beautiful laboratory of youth ministry.

Though I never could have said it then, I'm thankful today for that difficult summer when God first enrolled me into Soul School. I remember how the senior pastor at my church suggested that summer that I needed to attend a Graduate School of Character. Ouch! At the time I didn't appreciate his harsh critique of me, and I wanted to tell him he needed a few character classes of his own. (Actually, I had in mind a much more colorful way of saying it!) But I'm grateful that God used my pastor's challenge to introduce me to the School of the Soul, because I am still enrolled and plan to stay in classes for the rest of my life. This book is your invitation to sign up, to begin this journey of transformation, to start taking classes in Soul School. The tuition won't cost you a penny; but believe me, there is a price to be paid. But the reward is even greater.

So welcome to *Soul School*. Classes start now!

CHAPTER ONE

Be:Loved

Soul Lesson: Love must be the center from which all ministry flows.

Home improvement shows have a huge following these days. Viewers are captured by the astounding transformation that can take place within a single home in just a few short days. These shows make it look so simple—all you need are some materials from the local Home Depot, a free weekend, some capable and willing hands, and a vivacious host who runs around with a megaphone screaming your dreams into reality. Watching these shows, the average person might easily conclude that a whole home remodeling can really take place in seven short days. If only we saw behind the scenes—work crews of hundreds, pre-built materials delivered on huge trailers, thousands of dollars in supplies from a TV network hungry for ratings, and skilled editors who reshape seven days of hard work into an hour-long episode sure to inspire the would-be do-it-yourselfer.

I'm not sure if it was the influence of these shows, or just complete stupidity on the part of my husband and me, but we decided we'd seen enough episodes that we felt capable of renovating and finishing the basement of our first home. We'd just moved in to an adorable two-bedroom, one-bath, cottage-style home. It was cozy and charming, but lacking some good living space. So we decided to add a family room, a guest room, and a second bathroom to our unfinished basement. The only problem was that neither of us knew what we were doing. So we called upon the assistance and expertise of some friends and family whose toolboxes contained more than just a hammer and a tape measure.

One of those friends was a purebred Chicago plumber named Tom Digangi. Tom was the father of a student in the ministry my husband and I both worked with at our church. He told us he'd be willing to donate his time and rough in the basic plumbing if we'd do the rest of the labor. So we made a date for Tom to come over and jackhammer the concrete floor of our basement and lay down the pipe for the new bathroom. Jarrett and I made plans to be away from the house that day, since we knew we'd accomplish nothing worthwhile with the sound of a jackhammer in the background.

When we returned home that afternoon, we walked into an experience that's difficult to describe in the English language. As we stepped into our cute little cottage, the worst possible smell you can imagine infiltrated every pore in our bodies. The stench was unbearable. We didn't need any plumbing knowledge to know something had gone terribly wrong with Tom's project. Our belief that we were in a very bad situation was confirmed when we read Tom's note stuck on the back of our door: "CALL ME—IMMEDIATELY—TOM!!!!!"

Neither Jarrett nor I was brave enough to descend into our basement to investigate the odor, so we picked up our cordless phone, stepped into the hot July sun, and called our faithful plumber. When Tom picked up the phone, he immediately hit us with a statement you never want to hear from your plumber: "In my 20-some years as a plumber, I've never seen anything like what I found underneath your house." From the tone of his voice and the stench we'd just experienced, we knew the news wasn't good. Tom explained that the pipes beneath our foundation had been cracked for quite some time, and all the waste we'd flushed down our toilet over the past few years was just dwelling under our adorable cottage home. Tom assured us that he'd repaired the pipe, but that we'd be responsible for clearing away the waste and mud he'd had to shovel all over our basement floor. Yes, that's right, a mix of mud and real human waste was now in piles all around our basement.

I rarely play the "female" card in our marriage, but I'm no dummy. What lay ahead was not a job for me. So that night Jarrett and I bought every bottle of bleach available at the grocery store, suited up in boots, gloves, and masks, and tried to drown out the smell as best we could. But it would be his job to remove it from our basement the next morning.

Now the story could end here, and we'd all walk away with repulsive images of what was hanging out underneath our home. But in true youth ministry storytelling spirit, the tale only gets better. My wonderful husband spent the next day heroically shoveling our bleach-stained piles of waste-mud into "industrial strength" garbage bags to be hauled away. By the time I got home, Jarrett had filled 11 bags, and was just beginning to carry them out from our basement. As I walked down the stairs to check on my loving husband, I witnessed a scene that will never be removed from the annals of my mind. As Jarrett picked up two bags and flung them up onto his shoulders, those bags committed the crime of not living up to their "industrial strength." Both bags ripped simultaneously, pouring their contents all over him. My loving, kind, selfless husband stood there staring at me, a look of raw shock on his face. He was so besieged with disgust that he couldn't utter a word. He stood in silence for what seemed to be hours, covered in a grotesque combination of mud and human waste. There was nothing I could say to make the situation better—so for once in my life I just stayed quiet.

Years later, the story of installing a second bathroom in our home is an adventure we reminisce about with laughter (or at least I laugh). I'm happy to say that we no longer live in that home.

You may be wondering why I'd start a book about the state of our souls with such a story. Believe me, I contemplated whether it was wise for quite some time. But I keep coming back to a question I have found essential to living from my soul: *What lies beneath?* It's a fascinating question—and sometimes we need to take a jackhammer to the concrete foundation of our souls to find the answer.

We live in a world that's more interested in the surface. We focus on the outward qualities, because they're easy to detect. Digging down to the foundation can make a mess of your soul for a while, and processing what's found there can take lots of time and energy—two things that are not found in the abundance column of most youth workers' lives. But looking beneath the surface is essential to really knowing your soul and—more importantly—the One who created it.

Part of the problem is that many of us fear what we might find in the basement of our souls. We live as if we subconsciously believe that what lies beneath our foundation is no better than what we found under our basement that day. We know our stories and our skeletons, and we assume they make us too dingy to love. So we don't see ourselves as lovable. That's why so many of us spend absurd amounts of time living (and leading) from a place of conditions, rules, and self-induced policies. Because we don't see ourselves as lovable, we never truly believe we are loved—so we don't live as if we are loved.

In *Surrender to Love*, David Benner writes:

> Creation is an outpouring of love— an overflow from the heavens to earth. Creation not only declares the inventiveness and resourcefulness of God but reveals the abundance of his love. Creation declares that humans are born of love and for love, created in the image of a God who is love. Love is our source, and love is to be our fulfillment. Made in God's image, humans are invested with a nonnegotiable dignity. We are compatriots of God, not just creatures of God.

Benner's description reminds us that God's love for us is at our very core. The truest, purest, most essential piece of who we are is that we are loved. Simple and clean—our source is love. Our main ingredient is love. Our fulfillment and purpose is love—nothing more, nothing less. When God sees each of us, God sees love. So if you jackhammer your foundation, you won't find all kinds of garbage, waste, and refuse beneath the concrete. You may have to dig through layers of lies and rubble that have accumulated there, but the fullness of your identity, of my identity, is good old-fashioned love. What an incredibly liberating truth. From top to bottom, left to right, inside and out, we are loved. The breadth of you and me is love.

FRAGILE CHINA

As a teenager, Jenny was as fragile as a case of china. Her life was filled with screaming signals that she needed to be loved. She looked everywhere and anywhere for anything that even remotely resembled love. Jenny was a fabulous girl.

Outgoing, confident, a talented artist—she had so much to offer, yet couldn't see who she really was. She was convinced her foundation was a shaky pile of quicksand ready to devour her. Jenny believed she wasn't worth loving; therefore, she struggled to really love others.

Her story didn't help the process. Jenny had been shuffled from one parent to another for as long as she could remember. Both mom and dad had their own unique ways of triggering Jenny's insecurities. She desperately wanted her dad's approval. Like every child, Jenny longed to hear her dad say, "I'm so very proud of who you are." Her dad triggered Jenny's sense that she needed to perform for love. Jumping through hoops became a way of life for her.

With her mom, Jenny wanted some peace and stability. She watched her mom move from one husband to another. Each time her mom became dissatisfied with her current husband and moved on, Jenny paid the price. Jenny's sense of security was broken into a thousand pieces. Her mom made Jenny feel she was not important enough to love. She was overflowing with insecurity and was desperate for rest.

I first met Jenny at our summer camp. She was easy to pick out. She had an aura of pain surrounding her. During a time of worship one night, Jenny was overcome with anxiety. She walked out of the room where all our students were, and I happened to be in the hallway. Her eyes were flooded with tears, and her countenance was heavy. We sat down to talk, and Jenny began to unpack her suitcases of heartache, shame, and hurt. It was as if every time she heaved out another cry, the emptiness in her heart grew larger. It was clear that what she needed was to be loved. I am convinced the Holy Spirit prompted me that night with Jenny. Usually I say too much, and my words can resemble a bad fumble. But that night I was clear: The only words Jenny needed to hear were, "You are loved," "I love you," and "Jesus loves you." I didn't offer any counsel. I didn't ask any questions. I didn't pass any judgments on the predicament of Jenny's life. I just loved her. I held her; I cried with her; I comforted her. And somehow in that moment Jenny tangibly experienced that she was deeply loved by God. The love that was buried beneath began to seep up through the cracks in her foundation.

Jenny's life didn't turn around instantly. She had a long journey ahead of her—and still does. She was returning to a difficult situation. There were still deep wounds that would need to be unearthed. There were habits that needed to change. But that night, I watched Jenny slowly begin to embrace the truth that she was, without a doubt, loved, and maybe even more importantly, she was worth loving.

About a year and a half later, I had the privilege of baptizing Jenny. When we walked into the water, she handed me a piece of paper with the words "I am loved" written on it. Jenny got it. She knew she was loved, without a doubt.

I think the same delicate question Jenny struggled with is lingering somewhere in all of us. We might not have the same story as Jenny, but every human being at some point meets up with the inevitable question of worth. Our souls are wondering: Am I worth being loved? Part of the reason we ask the question at one point or another is because...we are all human. I know it sounds simple, but to be human is to want to be worthy of love.

IF ONLY

So many of us spend our days looking into gritty and murky mirrors that have camouflaged our identity as God's Beloved. I'm convinced that if we human beings all saw ourselves as God sees us, the world would be radically different. Most of us gaze into a reflection that is screaming back a list of things that need to be changed—a self-improvement agenda that even Dr. Phil wouldn't know what to do with.

If only I were more organized.

If only I were a better leader.

If only I hadn't messed up in the past.

If only I would stop failing.

If only I weighed less.

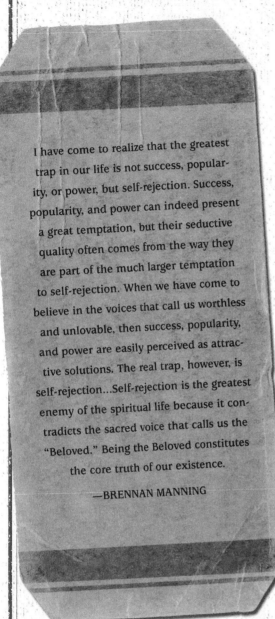

I have come to realize that the greatest trap in our life is not success, popularity, or power, but self-rejection. Success, popularity, and power can indeed present a great temptation, but their seductive quality often comes from the way they are part of the much larger temptation to self-rejection. When we have come to believe in the voices that call us worthless and unlovable, then success, popularity, and power are easily perceived as attractive solutions. The real trap, however, is self-rejection...Self-rejection is the greatest enemy of the spiritual life because it contradicts the sacred voice that calls us the "Beloved." Being the Beloved constitutes the core truth of our existence.

—BRENNAN MANNING

If only I made more money.

If only I were smarter.

If only I were married.

If only I were single again.

If only I had a bigger ministry.

If only I'd had different parents.

If only I were at a different church.

The worst thing about our *if onlys* is that they rob us of our ability to see our true identity as the Beloved. We're so busy trying to change ourselves (or at least wishing we were different) that we never embrace the simple fact that we are loved, just as we are. I'm not suggesting that we stop growing and maturing into the person we were created to be, but in order for us to have authentic mature growth, we need to embrace the truest aspect of who we are: We are loved. You can't do anything to be more loved. You are the beloved. The central truth and beauty that comes from living as a beloved child of God is that the word itself tells us all we have to do: *Be:Loved.* You and I need to *Be.* We need to stop trying to be loved. We need to just *Be...Loved.*

So how do we emerge from an existence of *if onlys?* The desperate question rattles through our locked up souls. Too many of us have grown up in a church culture that taught us that the only way to be free is to rid yourself of everything bad, sinful, and destructive in your life. Suffocate the sin, and then you will be able to breathe again. Kill the *if onlys,* and then you will really live. While eliminating everything undesirable from your life is a noble hope, I don't think it's a realistic possibility. The last time I checked humans were still sinful, and even a deep cleansing through the sin-removal spin cycle doesn't extract you from the category of being a sinful being.

Don't get me wrong: I'm all about confession, forgiveness, and renewal. But I would like to suggest that the process must include some realistic and healthy embracing of our fractured foundations. In fact, I'm suggesting that we start having funerals for our *if onlys*.

Funerals offer us an opportunity to remember the life of someone who has just died. Funerals give us opportunities to memorialize the life and influence of loved ones, to talk about the impact that they've had on us and the ways the world will be different without them. Over my years in ministry, I've been called upon to perform a number of funerals. It is not a task I enjoy. Weddings, graduations, baby dedications, birthday celebrations—I enjoy participating in all these events. But the passing of a life and memorializing a person's contributions to the world is something I will never find pleasant.

I once performed the funeral of a young man in our student ministry who was just a senior in high school when his life was tragically cut short by a brain tumor. David was smart, handsome, winsome, and outgoing—a great athlete and a devoted follower of Jesus.

I walked with David's family through the many months leading up to his death, and I was there on the morning of May 13 when he took his last earthly breath. It was an experience I will remember forever. In that moment, life changed instantly for David—he was finally released from his pain and began an eternity in heaven. But life also changed for David's family and friends. They would never again be the same. In a split second, a whole new life emerged for each of them—lives without the daily company of a son and brother and friend. These new lives were not given a warm welcome party, but they were their new lives nonetheless. David's funeral was a tribute to an all-too-short life well lived mixed with the perplexing question of "How do we move forward without David?"

When a loved one has died—someone who has played a momentous role in shaping who we are—how do we get used to a new life when that person is no longer with us? The only way I have learned is to take it one day at a time. Grief is an unpredictable and powerful emotion that has no rules. It takes on a life of its own. The process of learning how to live again after loss sometimes feels like you're walking round and round in circles instead of advancing to the other side. The loss of a loved and cherished person is always a subtraction from our lives, which almost always confronts us with the question of "How will I ever get used to living without this person?"

Similar questions confront us when we try to move ahead without the *if onlys* that have shaped us for so long. In a strange sort of way, it is essential that we acknowledge the profound influence our *if onlys* have had on our lives. We need to embrace the fact that they have affected how we live. They have changed the way we see the world, causing us to want to be different. But the reason we hold a funeral for our *if onlys* is that we don't want them to have power over us anymore. They need to be buried so new life can emerge. But our *if onlys* should never be forgotten. They should serve as a memorial of God's power in our lives.

Maybe your list of *if onlys* is connected to shame. You've quietly whispered to yourself, *"If only I hadn't done that."* Maybe you've lived with that shame for most of your life. It's played a main character in your story for far too long. You've learned how to feed it, hide it, live with it, and be ruled by it. Shame has found a permanent room in the basement of your soul. (It even makes its bed each day.) Maybe you've even gotten used to its company, but shame is not a house-guest that belongs in your soul. Beneath the basement of shame is a foundation of love.

Maybe your *if only* is connected to approval. You have lived your life telling yourself, *"If only I could get things right all the time, then I wouldn't feel like a failure, and people will love me for what I do."* You've become addicted to hearing applause, and you quietly seek it through every task you perform. You're so hungry for affirmation that it's become your motivation, robbing you of the pleasure that comes from serving.

To bury your *if onlys*, you need to acknowledge the role they've played in your life. Name the effects they've had on your relationships. Admit the ways they've directed your decisions. Accept that you are broken and in need of a Savior. Embrace your beautiful humanity as a reminder of grace.

We need to stop denying or ignoring our *if onlys*, and instead invite Jesus to replace them with love. We must ask for the courage to bury them and the hope and power to welcome a new life. The process of burying these things in our lives is no quick fix. A new and improved version of you won't just show up on your doorstep in four to six business days. But over time, by God's grace, your *if onlys* can be turned into *even thoughs*:

Even though there are days when you can't get it together and you feel out of control...
You are loved.

Even though it seems like everyone around you is disappointed in your performance...
You are loved.

Even though you feel like you're just a spiritual poser...
You are loved.

Even though you've traveled through life listening to lies about yourself, the truth is...
You are loved.

Even though you've learned how to numb the pain in your life with dangerous sedatives...
You are loved.

Even though you think you're too bad—or even too good...
You are loved.

Even though you've learned how to live from your head and suppress your heart...
You are loved.

Even though you live with a constant hunger for affirmation and affection...
You are loved.

Even though it feels like shame is the predominant fuel
running your life...
You are loved.

Even though your ministry sometimes runs on the fumes of an almost empty
soul...
You are loved.

A WHOLE NEW LIFE

Getting used to a new life without the *if onlys* that have played such a substantial role will take faith, hope, and love. There will be times when a memory or event will trigger a buried *if only*. We will probably quietly wonder if we will ever get used to living without the *if onlys* that have been with us so long. But be reminded that love lives in every crevice of your soul. There is no longer room for lies and deception—they've been buried. And one day at a time, we begin to see new life emerge. As Paul writes in the famous "love chapter" of 1 Corinthians:

> We don't yet see things clearly. We're squinting in a fog, peering through
> a mist. But it won't be long before the weather clears and the sun shines
> bright! We'll see it all then, see it all as clearly as God sees us; knowing
> him directly just as he knows us! But for right now, until that complete-
> ness, we have three things to do to lead us toward that consummation:
> Trust steadily in God, hope unswervingly, love extravagantly. And the best
> of the three is love.

—1 CORINTHIANS 13:12-14 (*The Message*)

Think of a newborn baby just beginning its adventure of living. For nine months her senses have only known darkness and warmth. She has only experienced safety and comfort. Then she is pushed through a painfully tight corridor and plopped into a new universe that is cold, bright, and loud. We are not much different when we leave our known existence of *if onlys* and enter into the freedom of *even thoughs*. We don't see things clearly right away. We squint through a fog of new possibilities. We are awakened to a liberation of hope. We hear the thunderous shouts of love that dissipate the past lies. Truth begins to prevail, clouds part, and love moves into town. The cracks in the foundation start to flood with truth. And then we start to see ourselves for who we really are. We start to live a life of knowing God, as he knows us. We start to trust God as our loving Father. We start to put our hope in his promises, and we begin to believe that his extravagant love is really for us.

This is the life of the Be:Loved.

Soul School Homework

Assignment

A task to be accomplished

Transforming *If Onlys* into *Even Thoughs*

Take a few minutes to list some of the internal and external *if onlys* in your life. What expectations do you place on yourself? What expectations do others place on you? Where do your feel pressure or stress? Where do you feel the need to perform? What lies have you believed about yourself that have contributed to your *if only* list? Try to be as honest and thorough as possible.

Example:

If only I were thinner then I would feel better about myself and people would show me more respect.

If only I had a supervisor that understood and encouraged my me then I would minister move effectively.

If only I...

If only I...

If only I...

If only I...

If only I...

Take some time to respond to each of your *if onlys* with a new *even though* statement of truth.

Example:
Even through I struggle with my weight and am not a supermodel, I am a beautiful, prized child of God, and I am loved.

Even though my supervisor does not speak love to me the way I desire to hear it, I choose to remember that I am valued, my work is important to God's kingdom activity, and I am loved.

Even though...

Even though...

Even though...

Even though...

Even though...

Lab

A place for practice and observation

Knock, Knock, Who's There?

Spend some time meditating on the following passage.

> "God is love. When we take up permanent residence in a life of love,
> we live in God and God lives in us. This way love has the run of the
> house, becomes at home and mature in us, so that we are free of
> worry on Judgment Day—our standing in the world is identical with
> Christ's."
>
> **—1 JOHN 4:17 (*The Message*)**

What words or phrases stand out to you in this passage?

How have you taken up permanent residence in a life of love? What practices or rituals in your life point to a life of love? Where do you need to grow in this area of your life?

Test

A procedure for critical evaluation; a means of determining the presence, quality, or truth of something; a trial

Be Listening to Love

Take the following test every day for the next week. Find a specific time and place in your home each day where you can spend 15 minutes communing with God. Let your only agenda in this time be to listen to God tell you that you are the Be:Loved. This is a silent exam. No grades will be given. The goal is to *Be*. Just listen to God remind you that you are the Be:Loved.

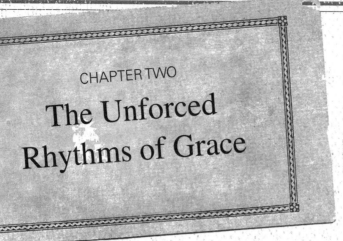

CHAPTER TWO

The Unforced Rhythms of Grace

Soul Lesson: Grace is the spiritual fuel that offers true freedom and peace.

CHECK GAUGE

We've all driven past the lonely guy walking alongside the road with his head hung low in frustration, body language screaming for all the world to hear that he has run out of gas. I know many times I've driven past with a sort of immature judgmental smirk thinking, *Sure stinks to be you,* while my gas light is flashing messages that if I don't fill up soon, I'll soon be joining that fellow on the same pavement of shame. I don't know why I feel the inclination to test my completely accurate fuel gauge that tells me I have exactly 4.6 miles before my car runs out of gas. But I confess that there have been far too many desperate pleading prayers during my many years of driving that sound something like, "Oh, God, please let there be a gas station at the next intersection. If there is, I will never let my car get beneath a quarter of a tank again. I promise."

I'm pretty sure the reason I keep finding myself in this predicament is that I've never run out of gas. I've never been the loser walking down the road with the gas can. So I keep going as long as I can. I think there's a twisted but playful part of me that feels like I've mastered the art of driving on fumes. The irony is that it makes me nervous every time I do it. I get tense and anxious. I look for other people to blame it on. ("If only my husband had filled up the car when he was last driving it.") I convince myself the fuel gauge is overly conservative in its warnings, and that I have 10 more miles than it's telling me. I hate driving on fumes, but I do it all the time.

Many of us do the same thing spiritually. We gamble with how long we can keep going before we run out of gas. We sometimes even do things that make it look like we're filling our tanks, but they're really just religious activities that drain us of real life. There have been seasons of my life when my exterior activity might suggest that I've never even dipped below half a tank. I work at a church, I counsel kids, I pray with people in need, I sign my notes with words like "Blessings" and "Because of Jesus"—and all the while I'm dangerously close to empty. I have learned to mask and ignore the flashing warning light that tells me I'm about to run out of gas.

I think many of the youth pastors I meet are caught in a cycle of continually "functioning on fumes" and never really getting filled up. So many of us are just plain tired. In fact, we are tired of being tired. For some, the exhaustion is physical—we're trying to function at a pace humanity was never intended for. For others, it's relational—we are trapped in a matrix of people who all need something from us. And for others, it's a soul exhaustion—our spirits are worn out. Many of us have existed on fumes for so long that we no longer realize it. We can't even imagine what it would feel like if our souls were filled to capacity.

WHAT WE ALL NEED

A while back I was in that all-too-common place of feeling terribly behind and overwhelmed by the number of tasks on my plate. I was responsible for overseeing student ministries at two different regional church campuses—and was about to take responsibility for a third that was getting ready to open its doors. During the previous two years, I'd started junior high and high school ministries at the two existing locations—each of which was 45 to 60 minutes from where I lived. I was responsible for finding venues, recruiting (sometimes begging) volunteers, hiring staff, giving talks, developing student-led worship bands, hauling equipment back and forth from campus to campus in a broken-down van, loving kids, communicating with parents, writing small group curriculum, and a hundred other things. Even though I had a great team of competent people who shared the load with me, I was tired. No, I was more than tired; I was worn-out—but I didn't want anyone to know how I was feeling. I wasn't willing to admit my need for rest because I was afraid I might be removed from the responsibility of remaining the leader.

As we prepared to launch ministries at our third site, I knew I needed someone to run our weekly programs, manage the creative process, work with our worship leaders, edit videos, and oversee our set-up and teardown team. It's an understatement to say that I was desperate to find that person. I'd almost reached a place where any warm-blooded Christian who loved students would do. A member of our team suggested I might want to contact a friend of his who was moving to the area, had a background in graphic design, and was very creative. I gave the guy a call, and we had a great conversation. The chemistry was good, he clearly had the capacity to do the job, and he'd worked with students in the past—so it was an easy decision. He was hired! Relief was in sight!

In our conversation I'd fished around to get a sense of his story and his character, but I didn't really do my normal deep dive into his interior life and the health (or lack of health) in his relationships with God and others. I liked him, and I was tired, so I decided he could do the job. No more questions needed. But our church wouldn't allow a staff person to be hired after just one phone call, so I set up some other phone calls and interviews so a few other people could help determine if he was right for the job. After interviews with several other members of my staff and some other leaders at the church, the consensus was that he'd have some things to learn but could probably do the job. He was recommended with slight reservation.

One of the final steps of the church's hiring process was for the candidate to meet with an elder. After the elder interview, I'd have the green light to offer the job. The elder who was doing the interview is wise, insightful, discerning, and honest. After she'd spoken with my potential hire, she called and we had a conversation about her findings. She affirmed that he had a lot to offer and probably could do the job, but she wanted to know if I knew about the unhealthy on-and-off relationship he'd been in with a former girlfriend over the past year. Not wanting to appear as if I hadn't asked him the tough question myself, I lied and said, "Yes." I lied to an elder. Well, I sort of knew about the relationship, but not the details. Honestly, I think I *wanted* to remain in the dark—I just wanted to hire him without a lot of hassles. As we continued talking, she began to discern that I didn't really know what she was talking about and very lovingly confronted me on it. I confessed to the lie I'd told and explained why. She forgave me and offered advice about how to proceed with the hiring.

The grace she offered was overwhelming to me. I didn't know what to do with it. I wanted to feel shame and guilt. I couldn't believe what I had done. But instead I felt loved, cared for, and believed in. Part of me was mortified that I'd made such a big mistake and then lied to cover it up—and another part of me was angry that those mistakes had been uncovered. But she offered me grace-filled support and forgiveness.

It's interesting that the grace I experienced from this wise elder was exactly what I needed to offer my potential hire. I called him and asked if we could meet. I apologized for not asking the harder questions earlier, and I began to dig into his story and his relationships. We toiled and tossed through some of the most difficult conversations I've ever experienced in an interview process. Together, we decided that he should still join the staff team, but that he needed to make some changes in his relationship with the woman that he had once dated.

Grace was the river that flowed through our conversation—and through our whole relationship. It didn't make the situation easy. There were still wise and appropriate boundaries that needed to be put in place. There were still whispers of doubt that troubled both of us from time to time. He sometimes felt he needed to perform perfectly without making any mistakes. I sometimes worried that any mistake he might make would draw more attention to my original error in hurrying the hiring. The situation offered both of us continuing opportunities to return to the river of grace.

I am so grateful that the story was written as it was. A number of years later, when I was moving on to a new ministry assignment, he wrote a letter to me that included the following words:

When I think back to the best and most growing times at Willow, they nearly always involve you in them. From dancing to Go-Go-Go Joseph at Sandblast to the meetings we had during my hiring process, the time was more fun and more growing than any I have known before. Your voice was always true. Your leadership and insight into my life brought clarity and calm. I have never worked under, and expect never to work under, a person who is more honest, passionate, and filled with as much soul as you. It has always been an honor to have worked with you. Your leadership is an inspiration and a hope that the church is capable of being something truly amazing.

His words were a tremendous gift and reminder that even in my most empty moments, God mysteriously and miraculously refills my tank. Jesus' invitation is to rest. To stop. To contemplate. To learn the unforced rhythms of grace:

> "Are you tired? Worn out? Burned out on religion? Come to me. Get away with me and you'll recover your life. I'll show you how to take a real rest. Walk with me and work with me—watch how I do it. Learn the unforced rhythms of grace. I won't lay anything heavy or ill-fitting on you. Keep company with me and you'll learn to live freely and lightly."
>
> **—MATTHEW 11:28-30 (*The Message*)**

If God's love is what lies beneath the foundation of our souls, then the fuel that keeps us functioning as the Beloved is grace—simple, pure, real, honest, forgiving grace. It's the absurd concept that has drawn most of us into an authentic relationship with Jesus. It is the free gift we are not worthy of receiving. It is the invitation to get away to a spiritual spa where your life is recovered, renewed, and redeemed not by any activity of your own. U2's Bono tells us, "Grace / She takes the blame / She covers the shame / Removes the stain." Grace is a never-ending fuel that offers compassionate freedom and rest.

MORE THAN A ONE-TRICK PONY

I'm not sure how I started thinking of grace as just a one-trick pony in my life. For far too long I limited grace to the single moment when I came to Jesus as a 13-year old girl and confessed that I needed a Savior. I naively thought my experience of receiving grace in that moment was so dramatic and complete that I didn't need to keep returning to the river where grace flows. But it's tough for me to imagine an idea that is more theologically backward—or more incongruent with what I've tried to teach and model in my own ministry.

As a youth worker I often find myself sitting across embarrassed kids as they tell me about the party they just went to, the lie they just told, the thing they just drank or smoked—and they are so ashamed it happened. My desire is always to remind them that their Friend and Savior Jesus never runs out of grace, and is always inviting them back to his side. I've sat across from parents who've discovered their child is involved in pornography and then felt them crumble into piles of guilt because they, too, are addicted to pornography—and the child learned the addiction from them. In that moment I never hesitate to embrace them and remind them that one of God's favorite things to do is get us cleaned up and offer a fresh start. I've worked with volunteers who feel compelled to step out of the ministry because of a deep moral sin in their lives. My desire is to love them, extend grace to them, and keep them engaged in the ministry in an appropriate role so they remain in a community of believers who will walk with them and extend God's refueling grace. I am always so eager to offer grace to others when they find themselves stalled on the side of the road with an empty fuel gauge. But when I look around and find that I'm the one on empty, I seem to come up with millions of excuses for why I don't deserve to pull into the same rest station where God longs to fill me with forgiveness, peace, and replenishment.

Too many youth workers are afraid to admit they're tired. Worn out. Insecure. Afraid. Lonely. Sinful. It's as if we youth workers wear a false badge of honor that says to be tired is to be successful. That working extra hard with unhealthy boundaries is spiritual. Since doing good things for God's kingdom and his people is what we are called to do, we think we need to buck up and keep going no matter the cost to our souls. We think that never admitting we need help is a good thing, that not relying on others communicates strength. Somehow we've come to believe that communing with God is good, but really *needing* God is bad.

I've been a resident of this camp, and I've seen the destruction it has done to my soul. I am grateful that God cares too much for our souls to allow us to stay here. Jesus, the inventor of grace, invites us to dwell in a very different place. The apostle Paul reminds us where we fit in the equation of grace:

> Now God has us where he wants us, with all the time in this world and the next to shower grace and kindness upon us in Christ Jesus. Saving is all his idea, and all his work. All we do is trust him enough to let him do it. It's God's gift from start to finish! We don't play the major role. If we did, we'd probably go around bragging that we'd done the whole thing! No, we neither make nor save ourselves. God does both the making and saving.

—EPHESIANS 2:7–9 (*The Message*)

A FULL TANK

Soon after I got my driver's license at age sixteen, my parents helped me purchase my first car. I'm pretty sure one reason they helped me get a car was so they could relinquish their parental taxi duties. I loved driving, and even more I loved the freedom that driving gave me, but I hated the responsibility of having to take care of my car. And, my bad habit of driving on fumes started as soon as I got the car. I would often go as long as possible without filling up my gas tank. There were many mornings when I would stay in bed until the last possible moment, battling my alarm clock for five more minutes of sleep, and then rush around with only minutes to get to school. Often, I would run out to the car, already late, knowing I hadn't filled the gas tank the night before, and I probably didn't have enough fuel to get me to school. I'd hop in my car and start it up—and the gas tank would be full. My dad had taken my car down the street and filled it up for me so I wouldn't have to do it. He would give me a completely full tank without my even asking for it. I don't know how many times this happened—but I know it was quite a few.

Maybe Dad is to blame for my perpetual habit of driving on fumes. But his kindness communicated to me how grace really works. Despite my irresponsibility, my dad didn't just lecture me on growing up and making sure the gas tank was full. He just filled it up.

That's the way grace works. You and I have nothing to do with it. God is the one who fills our tanks. All we have to do is trust him enough to start letting him fill us up.

Soul School Homework

Assignment
A task to be accomplished

Functioning on Fumes

Have you been functioning on spiritual fumes? Complete this assignment to help you determine where your spiritual fuel gauge is.

1. Do you feel like you are running from one thing to another and your spiritual connection with God gets pushed aside by all the busy activity?

Often				Sometimes				Never	
10	9	8	7	6	5	4	3	2	1

2. Do you find yourself rating your closeness to God according to the events in your life? (Examples: God just opened an opportunity for me in answer to my prayer...I feel close to him. God has not revealed to me what to do about a particular situation...I feel distant from him.)

Often				Sometimes				Never	
10	9	8	7	6	5	4	3	2	1

3. Do you find yourself feeling desperate for God when things get difficult, but allowing God to fade into a background role when life is going well?

Often				Sometimes				Never	
10	9	8	7	6	5	4	3	2	1

Reading the Fuel Gauge

Add up the numbers from the above questions _____

30 – 21 FUNCTIONING ON FUMES

You are probably functioning on fumes spiritually. Take some time NOW to determine how, where, and when you are going to spend time with God at his spiritual Fuel Station. Tell someone who loves you that your tank is nearing empty and you need support, prayer, and encouragement.

20 – 9 HALF -TANK

You are not empty, but you probably recognize areas of your life where you are spiritually tired and need to refuel with God. Make sure you setup regular times to be with God and connect to him in ways that refuel you.

8 – 3 FULL TANK

You have a full tank of grace. Find ways to offer encouragement to others who may be functioning on fumes or feeling empty. Stay connected to God and continue to be refueled by him.

Lab

A place for practice or observation

Casting Cares

Spend some time meditating on the following passage:

> Humble yourselves, therefore, under God's mighty hand, that he may
> lift you up in due time. Cast all your anxiety on him because he cares
> for you.
>
> —1 PETER 5:6–7

Make a list of the worries, burdens, or concerns you feel in your life right now. Pray through each one of them. Name them to God. Cast them on him. Ask him to take your burdens and to remind you of his care for you.

Test

A procedure for critical evaluation; a means of determining the presence, quality, or truth of something; a trial.

Fess Up

This week, find a loving person with whom you can share your spiritual fuel gauge. Tell that person your spiritual status—whether your tank is nearing empty, or just at a half tank, or feeling full. Ask for support, prayer, and encouragement.

CHAPTER THREE

Idol Eyes

Soul Lesson: Destruction of the idols in our lives is essential to authentic worship of the one true God.

I LIKE LADDERS BETTER THAN CHUTES

I was absolutely in love with my life—which, as Jesus reminds us, is a prerequisite to losing it.

Several years ago, the plot, set, characters, and script of the drama known as "Jeanne Stevens' life" seemed perfectly written for me. I was newly married to the man of my dreams. We were doing ministry together. I was working at an amazing church. I adored my job and the wonderful people with whom I was working. I lived in a fabulous city with family close by. I was using my spiritual gifts. I was gaining experiences that most people in their early twenties only dream of. The leaders in authority over me were taking notice and giving me encouragement and possibilities for advancement. I felt on fire. (Though I have plenty of issues, lack of confidence has never been one of them.) I was sure I'd found my stage in the church and that my play would be student ministry. And I was sure the plot would have me climbing the ladder to the very top.

Enter the problem. God isn't into rewarding those who seek to ascend into greatness. That's not the way God's economy works. Until that point my personal game of Chutes and Ladders had been all ladders; I was probably overdue for a good long slide back down a chute. My narcissism and manipulation were subtle, and I'd learned how to mask my need to be in control with spiritual language and religious activities. The student ministry that I was coleading had become a haven for my own self-absorbed agenda. I was aware that the purity of heart I'd once had for the church and student ministry had become clouded with my need to be important and influential. But I didn't want to take any action to change this, because I knew it would require a painful sacrifice and shift in how I was living.

I knew something—or maybe even someone—was standing in the way of how God wanted me to live. But I never would have dreamed I had an issue with worshipping idols.

NO, NOT ME

I'd always thought of idol worship as a sin reserved for pagan people in faraway places. My image of idol worship was that scene in *Indiana Jones and the Temple of Doom* when the priest reaches into a man's chest and removes his heart as an offering for the pagan god Mahakali. I've never forgotten how the priest allowed the man and his still-beating heart to erupt in flames of sacrificial worship.

So it was quite alarming to hear my spiritual mentor tell me that I was not really worshiping God but engaging in idol worship. "Hold up," I wanted to say. "You are my mentor. I'm here because I wanted you to help me better connect with God, and now you're telling me I'm not even worshipping God?" After all, I'm a youth pastor. I'm employed by the church. I went to a Bible theology school. How could she be suggesting I was an idol worshipper?

Of course, I could easily see the idols that my students worship. They make idols out of fashion and sports and popularity and school and even each other. But not me. Yet I felt an internal alarm ringing inside that told me what she was saying was true. I just didn't want to admit it. Obviously, I didn't have a golden cow with candles around it down in my basement. I love God, Jesus is my redeemer, and the Holy Spirit is the guiding force helping me through my journey. But I had started to put a few other people and things ahead of God on the altar where I worshipped. I couldn't imagine going public with this kind of sin. What would people think of a youth pastor who didn't really worship God?

There's no question that we live in a culture and society obsessed with all sorts of idols. The idol of money and material possessions. The idol of relationships. The idol of power and control. The idols of food, alcohol, and drugs. The idol of narcissism—wanting to do life according to your desires on your clock. You get the point: Idol worship is not just an Old Testament problem; it's very much a today problem. But I think those of us who work in full-time ministry or volunteer at the church tend to think we escape with a free pass on this one. In fact, maybe you looked at the title of this chapter and thought, "Here's a section I don't need to read. This is not an issue in my life." Maybe—and if that's the case, then great. But I invite you to indulge me for just a few more moments and see if you've ever encountered any of these "golden cows" during your journey of working with students.

YOUTH MINISTRY GOLDEN COWS

Has there ever been a moment when you've reached the end of your program or gathering and felt disappointed with the number of students who showed up? Maybe you were even tempted to exaggerate the number of kids who were really there. Do you ever notice that you tend to feel good about your ministry only if you get positive feedback from someone—but if you get an e-mail from a disappointed parent, then your general attitude about the ministry is bad? Do the comments, suggestions, and opinions of others have a disproportionate bearing on your decision-making and your ability to listen to what God is saying to you about the ministry? **Maybe EXTERNAL SUCCESS is your idol.**

Have you ever had weeks where it seems like every single moment finds you in a hurry? Off to the next meeting, always five minutes behind, trying to juggle a bunch of tasks you should never have agreed to do, disappointing people important to you, and constantly injecting yourself with caffeine just so you have energy to make it through the day. Do you ever feel like you can't function if you leave your cell phone or calendar at home? Do people regularly start their conversations with you by saying, "I know you're *so* busy..."? Could it be that you've made constant activity more important than the actual ministry you've been called to do? **Maybe BUSYNESS is your idol.**

Have you ever listened to other youth workers describing their ministries and realized you're spending all your time comparing their efforts with what you are doing in your own ministry or small group? Do you find yourself judging their intentions, wondering if their ministries are really deep and helpful, or if it's just good snacks, good music, and funny stories that keep students coming back? Are you inclined to downplay the work of others—even when you don't really know what's going on with them—just to make yourself feel better about what you're doing? Could it be that your insecurity and fear of failure have become more important than the God who created you and called you to a unique purpose? **Maybe COMPARISON is your idol.**

Have you ever found yourself wishing you could just go back to the "good old days"—when you were younger and loved your job, felt freedom in what you were doing, felt like you were in control, and everything just seemed to work? Could it be that you're more focused on the past than the ways God wants to use you in the present? Or have you ever found yourself wishing you could fast-forward out of your present reality? As soon as we get past this dry spell, things will be better. As soon as we make this staffing change, strategy change, small group change, senior pastor change—*then* we will be on a roll. **Maybe LIVING IN THE PAST or WISHING FOR THE FUTURE is your idol.**

Have you ever felt like you just can't possibly be a part of one more ministry at the church? Your volunteering has become a full-time job, or your full-time church work has taken over your life? Maybe you're frustrated that your students don't know God's Word. You've put a ton of time into teaching the Bible and trying to get youth interested in theology, and you feel like a broken record that is constantly urging them to serve the poor, have a quiet time, show up at church, make sure you invite a friend who doesn't know Jesus, etc., etc., etc. Could it be that you're making the constant activity of church work more important than the practice of growing and developing an authentic relationship with God? **Maybe RELIGIOUS ACTIVITY is your idol.**

Have you ever looked at your bookshelf and realized you own almost every youth ministry book ever written? Your calendar is jam-packed with all the different

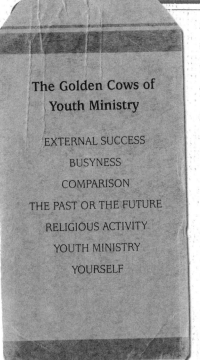

The Golden Cows of Youth Ministry

EXTERNAL SUCCESS

BUSYNESS

COMPARISON

THE PAST OR THE FUTURE

RELIGIOUS ACTIVITY

YOUTH MINISTRY

YOURSELF

conferences. You feel most comfortable with other people who are connected in the youth ministry world. You know every game by heart. You're always working on a funny illustration to drive home a point. Do you find you're making all your deposits into what you're doing with the youth group while the rest of your life is overdrawn? **Maybe YOUTH MINISTRY itself is your idol.**

Have you ever found yourself praying prayers that are more informational agendas of how you want life to function vs. listening to God's desire for your life? Do your needs and desires always seem to be more important than others? Do you find yourself never taking blame for the problems that arise in your ministry; it's always something or someone else's fault? Is there a low-grade fear that lives in you that always wants to make sure that you get what you need and receive the recognition that you deserve? **Maybe YOU, YOURSELF are the idol you are worshiping.**

If you didn't relate to anything in the scenarios above, then I'd invite you to jump to the next chapter—and please call me some time and tell me what it's like to walk on water. But I suspect at least some of these struggles will feel familiar to most youth ministers. There are surely other idols I've not mentioned (and the ones above have lots of different forms and faces), but these are some of the ones I've recognized most in the world of youth ministry—perhaps because they are the ones I've recognized most in myself. Many of us in youth ministry have invisible altars that define who and what we truly worship, driving our intentions, decisions, and actions. We are called to a life of having no gods other than the one true God, yet we continue to bow before a wide variety of golden cows.

You don't have to turn too far into the pages of Scripture to see idolatry. The very first sin in the Bible is a form of idol worship. Adam and Eve were not content with who they were and all God had given to them. They selfishly wanted to be like God, so they put themselves ahead of their maker and yanked the apple from that tree. The second they bit into that Granny Smith they made their desires more important than God, thereby making themselves an idol. Anytime we put someone or something ahead of God, we worship an idol.

Flip to the book of Exodus and you find God speaking these words:

> "I am the Lord your God, who brought you out of Egypt, out of the land
> of slavery. You shall have no other gods before me. You shall not make for
> yourself an image in the form of anything in heaven above or on the earth
> beneath or in the waters below. You shall not bow down to them or wor-
> ship them; for I, the Lord your God, am a jealous God."

—EXODUS 20:2–5

God made it extremely clear: He has an issue with jealousy. It's not like the kind
of immature jealousy where a guy doesn't want his girlfriend talking to another guy.
It's the kind of healthy jealousy that the Maker of the universe holds to in refusing to
share his altar with our self-made idols. Even though God has made clear his desire
for the human race, our tendency to place value on some-
thing or someone in a way that rivals the love and affection
that belongs only to God stains the story of humanity from
Genesis to Revelation. From the earliest biblical times to
today, people have been bowing down to the false gods
they've made for centuries. So who are we to think we
aren't capable of slipping into idol worship? And if we
discover these idols in our lives...what do we do? This is
the question I found myself asking.

Pop Quiz

Is there someone or something
in your life that is receiving the
love and affection that rightly
belongs only to God?

FACING THE FIRE

I wasn't even sure how I'd ended up at the altars of these false gods. I knew it wasn't
a road I'd chosen intentionally, but nonetheless I was there—and I was eager to find
my way back to the one true God. And I knew that the only way to the altar of the one
true God would be through the serious route of sacrifice—sacrifice of my false gods.

So if you're serious about living this new resurrection life with Christ, act like it. Pursue the things over which Christ presides. Don't shuffle along, eyes to the ground, absorbed with the things right in front of you. Look up, and be alert to what is going on around Christ—that's where the action is. See things from his perspective.

—COLOSSIANS 3:1–2 (*The Message*)

God was asking me to sacrifice my false gods. He was calling me to stop shuffling along through a self-absorbed life of good appearances with manipulative intentions. God wanted my sacrificial worship of him and him alone. For me that meant sacrificing the gods of ministry and myself. I had cozied myself into a comfy corner of control and started to believe the lie that I could be in charge of my life. I'd made my own desires more important than God and his direction for my life. My ministry had become focused on what I could do and who would notice me doing it.

My heart had once leaped with the love of God and his church. It was a desire to help kids grow in their faith that had drawn me into ministry. I used to feel almost giddy if I saw a group of students worshipping. But my heart was growing cold and predictable. My prayers were flat and selfish. The life I'd once loved living was not attractive anymore. Something had to change—rather, something needed to be destroyed. The idols of "me" and "ministry" needed to be sacrificed in the fire. But I was no fool. I knew that if I threw myself and my love of ministry into a raging fire, there was no promise that God would pull out his old trick and save me from the fiery furnace like Shadrach, Meshach, and Abednego. In fact, I

Jeanne, I have taken you through a fire. It was quite fierce. You are now a burn victim. You have been forever affected. You will never forget the heat and pain of the flames. You may forget some of the specifics of the when and how, but you will never forget how this fire has changed your life. I do not view the fire as a tragedy. I see it as a victory. Jeanne, you were not consumed by the fire. The fire did not defeat you. It purified you. It brought healing to you. The fire allowed trust to make a permanent residence in you. You walked where I wanted you to go, and I never left you. The fire put me back on the throne in your life.

was pretty sure that walking into that fire would be hot, uncomfortable, and most likely would leave some scars. My greatest fear was not knowing what life would be like on the other side. I'd become quite comfortable managing my life and ministry, and I was afraid God would radically rearrange everything I'd gotten so neatly in place. But I knew I had no other choice.

So one evening I started a roaring fire in our fireplace. I took a piece of paper and began writing out the idols I had created and how they had taken places of prominent position in my life. I painstakingly wrote down every detail I could recall about how I'd put myself and my ministry above God. I read them aloud, and then ceremoniously tossed them into the flames, offering them as sacrifice to my one true God.

I wish I could tell you that everything went perfectly for me from that moment on. But the season that followed was one of the hardest times of my life. My life started to shift in directions that were beyond uncomfortable. I felt I was descending. I felt out of control. I was vulnerable and needy. I lost a ministry position at the church. My once shiny reputation felt like it had a mammoth scarlet letter over it. I felt misunderstood. Unappreciated. Insecure. The fire was much worse than I'd expected. And there was a part of me that felt like walking into that consuming fire was the biggest mistake of my life. I have many, many journal entries from that time that are filled with desperate prayers begging God to turn down the heat. Being a worshipper of the one and only God sent me into a tailspin of being completely out of control. But my giving up control is exactly what needed to happen.

Many years later, while writing in my journal, I felt God asking me to write myself a reminder about the importance of the sacrificial fire. I felt like God was urging me to write it in his words, as a note to myself. Here are the words I was hearing God say to me:

Maybe you're like I was, and didn't expect to find anything in a chapter on idols that would relate to your life. Perhaps you read this chapter only because you like to read a book from beginning to end and skipping something in the middle would throw you off. Or maybe you read it because it sometimes feels good to see that someone else in the world is more messed up than you are. (Hey, wait a minute. That would be me who you think is messed up...) But maybe there are some idols on the altar of your life and you can hear the one true God beckoning you to the sacrificial fire. You smell the kindling burning; you can hear the wood crackling. You know where you need to go. So go to the fire where you can sacrifice your idols to the living God. And take heart in the knowledge that our God is a consuming fire of love.

> Therefore, since we are receiving a kingdom that cannot be shaken, let us be thankful, and so worship God acceptably with reverence and awe, for our "God is a consuming fire."

—HEBREWS 12:28-29

Soul School Homework

Assignment
A task to be accomplished

Identify Your Idols

Refer back to the descriptions and questions in the chapter for each of these "Youth Ministry Golden Cows." Circle the ones with which you struggle the most.

EXTERNAL SUCCESS

BUSYNESS

COMPARISON

THE PAST OR THE FUTURE

RELIGIOUS ACTIVITY

YOUTH MINISTRY

YOURSELF

Spend some time writing out the ways these idols are at work in your life. Try to be as clear and specific as possible.

Example: *My idol is Comparison. I constantly measure myself against other people. I even judge others so I can appear to be better. Here are the specific ways Comparison controls my life.....*

Lab
A place for practice or observation

Destroy Your Idol

Find a place where you can start a fire. (A safe place—like a fireplace or a fire pit. I don't want to be responsible for the fire department coming to your home!) Take the sheet of paper where you've defined your idol and read it aloud to God. Don't hold back any details—God already knows how the idol has affected your life. Confess your desire for God to sit on the throne of your life. Ceremoniously offer that idol to the one true God. Throw the piece of paper into the fire and watch God destroy the idol as he consumes your life in love.

Test
A procedure for critical evaluation; a means of determining the presence, quality, or truth of something; a trial

Worship the One True God

Spend some time in private worship of the one true God. Sing to him. Pray to him. Bless him. Honor him. Thank him. Turn on a favorite worship CD and sing your heart out. Or go for a walk in his creation and thank him for its beauty. Or write an original Psalm to him. Take time to intentionally worship your ONE TRUE GOD.

> Come, let us sing for joy to the Lord;
>
> let us shout aloud to the Rock of our salvation.
>
> Let us come before him with thanksgiving
>
> and extol him with music and song.
>
> For the Lord is the great God,
>
> the great King above all gods.
>
> In his hand are the depths of the earth,
>
> and the mountain peaks belong to him.
>
> The sea is his, for he made it,
>
> and his hands formed the dry land.
>
> Come, let us bow down in worship,
>
> let us kneel before the Lord our Maker;
>
> for he is our God
>
> and we are the people of his pasture,
>
> the flock under his care.

—PSALM 95:1–7

SECTION TWO

Settling In

When Jesus arrived in the villages of Caesarea Philippi, he asked his disciples, "What are people saying about who the Son of Man is?" They replied, "Some think he is John the Baptizer, some say Elijah, some Jeremiah or one of the other prophets." He pressed them, "And how about you? Who do you say I am?" Simon Peter said, "You're the Christ, the Messiah, the Son of the living God." Jesus came back, "God bless you, Simon, son of Jonah! You didn't get that answer out of books or from teachers. My Father in heaven, God himself, let you in on this secret of who I really am. And now I'm going to tell you who you are, really are. You are Peter, a rock. This is the rock on which I will put together my church, a church so expansive with energy that not even the gates of hell will be able to keep it out.

—MATTHEW 16:13–18 (*The Message*)

I love this passage of Scripture. Part of the reason is the delightful and imaginative humor that comes across in this tale of the Savior of the universe asking his buddies what the word on the street is about his reputation. The thought of Jesus trying to find out what was written about him in the bathroom stalls reminds me of my awkward days in junior high, when I was battling through the murky swamp of adolescence—desperate to know who I was but even more desperate to know what others thought of me. I am grateful that the majority of the identity turmoil I experienced in adolescence has passed. But I still find myself deeply curious about the question Jesus posed.

I am confident Jesus was not wondering about who he was. But I believe his willingness to thoughtfully engage in one of the deepest questions of humanity grants each of us permission to ask the same question. So following Jesus' spirit and example, I have been asking, "Who do you say I am, Jesus?"

This question has been one of the primary propelling forces that have helped me identify my true self and my purpose on the planet. As I have wrestled with the complicated realities surrounding such a question, I have realized that living out of my truest identity is one of the greatest ways I can love God with all of my heart, soul, mind, and strength. But I have also realized that committing myself to living out of my truest identity is one of the most difficult and complicated decisions I will ever make.

The fight for a true identity begins for each of us on the day we are born. To be the unique creations we were created to be gets complicated early on. As David Benner says, "Body and Soul contain thousands of possibilities out of which we can build many identities." We often vacillate between our true selves and our false selves. We wear masks in an attempt to cover our insecurities and vulnerability. If only we knew exactly who we were at every given moment.

Many of us have built wardrobes full of false identities we've become too comfortable in wearing. To enroll in the School of the Soul will require a cleaning of the closet. To become the unique you God has created you to be is one of the greatest and most challenging quests of your life. But there is only one you, and no one else can ever play the unique role God has designed for you alone.

In all of creation, identity is a challenge only for humans. A tulip knows exactly what it is. It is never tempted by false ways of being. Nor does it face complicated decisions in the process of becoming. So it is with dogs, rocks, trees, stars, amoebas, electrons, and all other things. All give glory to God by being exactly what they are. For in being what God means them to be, they are obeying him. Humans, however, encounter a more challenging existence. We think. We consider options. We decide. We act. We doubt. Simple being is tremendously difficult to achieve and fully authentic being is extremely rare. Body and Soul contain thousands of possibilities out of which we can build many identities."

—DAVID BENNER,
THE GIFT OF BEING YOURSELF

CHAPTER FOUR

Performers, Pleasers, & Protectors

Soul Lesson: "Performer," "Pleaser," and "Protector" are roles we adopt when we're young, and many of us have mastered these parts. But these roles keep us from the true spiritual power available to each of us when we exchange them for our rightful role as a Son or Daughter of God.

WHEN I GROW UP...

As a child I had all sorts of dreams of what I would be when I grew up. But none of those visions ever included me sitting in a circle of uncomfortable folding chairs in a bland room with the pungent smell of stale coffee, choking back a confession that I am an addict.

I'm trying to remember where my particular addiction really started. It could have been when I played the part of Evil Alice Acid in our third-grade play, "Tilly the Tooth" (our teacher's noble and creative attempt to educate us eight-year-olds about healthy oral hygiene). Or maybe it was at my first piano recital, when I made it through my performance of "The Little Wigwam" without any mistakes. Or maybe it was when I was writing, directing, and producing my own backyard plays (in which I also had the starring role, of course). But somewhere along the line I started to become addicted to the glorious sound elicited when two hands come together repeatedly in a rhythmic beat. I loved when people applauded what I was doing. I felt most alive when I was performing. Little did I know that I was developing a destructive addiction in my soul that would one day be very difficult and painful to overcome.

Even though there are not PPPA (Performers, Pleasers, & Protectors Anonymous) meetings all over the country, there are lots of Performers and Pleasers and Protectors who are dying to get out of the cycle of the empty selves they are living in. What's even more alarming to me is just how many of us are in youth ministry. Perhaps it's because our youth groups were the first safe place where our gifts were encouraged and used for good. Or maybe it's because each of these roles is rooted in some good quality that becomes distorted. For example, we all have a desire for encouragement and affirmation. But maybe we find that our once-healthy longing for affirmation has started to turn desperate, and we've grown into Performers. Youth ministry is also a place where there are lots of needs. Very few youth ministries have the luxury of turning volunteers away. Many of us got involved with youth ministry because we love to help and pitch in toward a good cause. But that noble and pure desire to serve God and others can sometimes sour as we learn how to meet needs and keep others satisfied, and the Pleaser is born. Youth ministry can also be a place where we are affirmed as we are. Such acceptance is a good thing. But when no one challenges us, when no one pushes us to risk, we can fall into the false comfort of being a Protector. Whatever the situation, youth ministry seems like a magnet that draws those of us who need to work out our performing and pleasing and protecting selves.

I remember a time when I realized I was smack dab in the middle of a ministry position loaded with potential for me to continue down the addictive and destructive path of living as a PPP. After admitting the danger to myself, my natural and extremist inclination was to jump into a thorough spiritually bleaching spin-cycle to rid myself of my performing, pleasing, and protecting ways. But God lovingly and firmly helped me see that the process of transformation was not going to be one of brutal self-rejection and self-sanitizing. Instead, it would be one of embracing and integrating my false selves into a more complete me. It was a long process of deep introspection, honest conversations with a mentor, confessions to a safe community, and lots and lots of time.

Even though there were parts of me that wanted to hide and deal with my "false self issues" in private, at the time it was sadly comforting to look around the world of youth ministry and recognize I had lots of company. Youth ministries are overflowing with Performers, Pleasers, and Protectors—from the paid professional to the volunteer small group leader to the parent opening her home and paying for the pizza. PPPs are everywhere, but most of us are masters at camouflaging our addictions amidst lots of spiritual activity. Sometimes we hide these addictions so well we can't even see them ourselves! So just in case you are another PPP like me who has become proficient at shrouding your addiction, I've decided to make it explicitly clear about how PPPs have become embedded into the culture of youth ministry. What follows are my own nonclinical and non-*Webster's Dictionary* definitions (translation: they are neither exhaustive nor complete). You may feel like you identify with all of these definitions or just one of them:

- Performers look for affection and affirmation in the applause of others. They live in a continuous cycle of trying to outshine everyone else. Sometimes the Performer is called a perfectionist. The need to achieve is often the addiction that drives Performers to cover up the deep insecurities that linger within.

- Pleasers learn how to adapt themselves to the expectations of others. They learn what others want to hear and how they want to hear it. People love a Pleaser.

- Protectors work hard to keep themselves away from any possible disappointment. They protect their feelings. They rarely take risks. They stick with what is known and what keeps them feeling safe. Often they are pessimistic about possibility and potential.

A YOUTH MINISTRY CULTURE OF PPP

Performers: What gets applauded in youth ministry and why?

Big Things: When lots of kids show up regularly, others assume and often say, "God must really be at work in your youth ministry!" When we do an overnight retreat or oversee an out-of-this-world mission trip, we turn up the volume and make sure everyone hears that big things are happening in the youth ministry. Why do we do it? Because when the external signs point to success, we don't have to focus on the flaws we're desperately trying to cover up. No one wants to talk publicly about the volunteers who have left the ministry. No one likes to highlight the kids who sit on the back wall week after week and don't feel welcome. No one likes to admit that their small groups usually feel more like gossip sessions than Bible studies. Big numbers and noticeable events give the impression that all is well in the youth ministry and often conceal our inner fear that our ministries may be shallow or spiritually ineffective.

Pop Quiz

With which of these roles do you struggle most: Performing, Pleasing, or Protecting?

Salvation: When one of the students in your ministry becomes a Christian, the fireworks go off—and well they should.

When a life is saved and redeemed, when an eternal reservation is made in heaven, all the angels celebrate, and we should too. But we all know that for most Christians, the moment of salvation is the easiest moment of the Christian life. It's the following, the growing, the fumbling-and-getting-up-again that is the real challenge, yet we rarely celebrate when someone is being faithful in their day-to-day spiritual life. I think many of us have taken the wondrous and miraculous moment of salvation and turned it into a report card. When lots of students raise their hands, come forward at the end of the service, check that they've offered a prayer accepting Christ—or however you identify a profession of faith—we give ourselves an A+. But when the youth ministry is just clicking along and students are making daily choices to honor God in their everyday lives, many of us give ourselves a C- (at best) and start wondering what's wrong. Why aren't students finding Jesus? Too often, we're excited only when we're seeing new converts. We quantify daily faithfulness and obedience as normal and boring.

Up-front Gifts: When we see kids who are good in front of a crowd, we scoop 'em up and put 'em on stage. We give leadership responsibilities to the outgoing, confident students while we offer the more reserved students the behind-the-scenes tasks. Youth ministries have become training camps that encourage an unhealthy hierarchy of spiritual gifts. We send subtle and sometimes overt messages that certain gifts are far more important in God's kingdom. We celebrate gifts like leadership and teaching but often brush over gifts like mercy and service. I think many of us pass on these messages because we're operating in adult church cultures afflicted by the same disease.

Slick Programs: When the program goes well—the sound is dialed in, the video works, the worship is inspiring, and the message has people rolling in the aisles with laughter, then weeping with conviction—we say it was successful. Many of us have become experts at piecing together an hour-long experience that will speak to the felt needs of students. But I wonder if we've packed our cue sheets so tight with dazzling elements that we leave no room for God—what if he took too much time with his message? I love a well-crafted program that helps communicate God's love and truth, but I think many of us spend far too much time planning the programs while the rest of the ministry is falling apart. We applaud the slick programs because they are noticeable, but they are usually not where real spiritual fruit buds and grows.

Pleasers: Who are we trying to make happy and why?

Authority Figures: Many of us have become proficient at figuring out and then supplying exactly what our leader, senior pastor, or boss wants from us. We know their definitions of success, and we are determined to give it to them. We don't want to be the mediocre youth pastor or volunteer, so we do whatever we can to stand out and make our authority figure happy. Some of us become slaves to the voices of our leaders because we don't trust our own intuitions and ideas. Others don't want to rock the boat, so we settle into the role of a faithful worker bee. Others are in toxic situations that feel more like a military command than a ministry, and decide out of fear to submit and stay silent. Honoring a leader or authority figure is noble and right, but pleasing and playing to an authority figure can be destructive to the leader's ego and the follower's sense of self. In these situations both parties lose.

Peers: We know all about the peer pressure adolescents face. But even though we no longer face the same pressure many of us felt in our teenage years, I've watched countless youth workers change ministry directions because of what some other youth minister was doing. Youth workers are notorious for wanting to create "holy dittos"—copies of what has been successful in another ministry. If it worked for some other small group leader or youth minister, we figure it'll probably work for us. We start to become Pleasers of our peers by copying them.

Parents: The theme song for many youth ministries could be "When You're Good to Mama" from the Broadway musical *Chicago*. I love the last line of the song, "So what's the one conclusion / I can bring this number to? / When you're good to Mama

/ Mama's good to you!" Parents are usually the biggest critics of a church's youth ministry. If their 14-year-old son is found smoking, it's the youth ministry's fault. But when the 15-year-old girl sees someone sitting alone in the school cafeteria and sits down to eat lunch with that person, the youth ministry rarely gets acknowledged. Parents tend to speak up when things aren't going well, and many youth workers have become skilled defensive and even offensive players in the ongoing game of trying to please the parents of our adolescents. We try to keep the parents happy, and when they aren't, we start changing everything around in hopes of winning back their approval and support. We become Pleasers of parents instead of partners with them, in the belief that if we're good to them, they'll be good to us.

Kids: No youth worker wants to feel like the loser adult the students aren't interested in. Maybe that's why so many of us have started rearranging how we look and act so students think we're cool. I was amused as I walked around a recent youth workers' conference and noticed how trendy and fashionable the youth workers were. Please don't get me wrong: I am not knocking personal preference when it comes to apparel. I have my fair share of Pumas and track jackets in my closet. But as I gazed at the sea of youth workers who look like bigger versions of their students, I began to wonder if some youth workers are trying too hard to please our students. Do we sometimes compromise who we really are so our students will accept us?

"Tapes" from the Past: Some of us spend our present ministries trying to right the mistakes of the past. It's not uncommon for youth ministers to have a collection of old tapes echoing through the corridors of our minds, filling us with messages that take us back to moments we wish we could forget. We regret some pain we once caused or struggle with some verdict that was pronounced on us. The content and voices found on these old tapes will be different for each of us, but some youth ministers spend tons of time and energy trying to please (and appease) voices and moments that have nothing to do with their present.

Ourselves: Many of us are obsessed with an internal voice that drives us. We have expectations about who we are and what we need to become. I have talked with so many different youth workers who are plagued by unrealistic expectations about themselves and how they need to live. They've become prisoners of their own high standards and their need to please themselves.

Protectors: What are we trying to guard and why?

Ego: Many youth workers have become professional Protectors because they dread the thought of ever having to admit defeat. The mere possibility of failure sends some leaders into a panic of wanting to safeguard themselves and their egos. So they start to play it safe in their relationships and their ministries. There are far too many youth workers who put forth a shiny veneer of security and self-confidence while fighting inside to protect themselves from their own fears and doubts.

The Way It's "Always" Been Done: You might not think youth ministry has a long enough history to make us nostalgic and reminiscent of the good ol' days. But many youth workers refuse to move forward because they feel more comfortable with how they've always done things. They stay stuck in a past that no longer speaks to the present tensions of youth culture. Their fear of not being relevant keeps them in a posture of protecting.

Exposure: I have a friend who volunteers in the youth ministry at his church. He possesses many awesome qualities that make him a great small group leader. His middle school guys love him. He is fun, energetic, and consistent in their lives, and he genuinely loves Jesus. But his relational world is a mess. He tries to keep it covered up for fear he might be found out. He has a broken relationship with his parents, he has a long line of ex-girlfriends, and he burns through friends quicker than a group of middle schoolers polishing off a box of Krispy Kreme doughnuts. He knows his relational world needs some focused attention and improvement. But instead of bringing it out into the open, he keeps it hidden and protected. This desire to cover up our problems rather than deal with them is fairly common among youth pastors. The thought of being exposed for who we really are causes us to become Protectors.

OVERCOMING OUR PPP ADDICTIONS

For each of us, the honest recognition of our tendency to become Performers, Pleasers, and Protectors can be a very difficult experience. As I said earlier, when I see things in myself that are disappointing or realize I'm not living the way God fully intended, my first response is usually one of extreme intolerance. I try to shed any connection I might have toward the behavior that concerns me. While there is wisdom in denying tendencies toward unhealthy living, I found that God was not asking me to discard components of who I am. Instead, God wanted to walk me toward a more fully integrated me. I have seen, in my own life and many others, the fruit that comes from fully yielding all that we are to Jesus—including our PPP addictions. Listen to Jesus' words:

> "I am the true vine, and my Father is the gardener. He cuts off every
> branch in me that bears no fruit, while every branch that does bear fruit
> he prunes so that it will be even more fruitful...I am the vine; you are the
> branches. If you remain in me and I in you, you will bear much fruit; apart
> from me you can do nothing. If you do not remain in me, you are like a
> branch that is thrown away and withers; such branches are picked up,
> thrown into the fire and burned."
>
> **—JOHN 15:1-2, 5-6**

Jesus isn't asking us to connect only the holy and healthy aspects of who we are to him. He wants all of us—including every possible true and false self—to be connected to all of him. His invitation to remain in him is complete and all-inclusive. He doesn't want a divided self. When we are completely connected to Jesus, the true vine, our lives will bear much fruit. But apart from complete connection, our lives are nothing. Too many of us feel spiritually lifeless because we keep our full humanity detached from the vine. We live in fear that God is going to throw our ugly selves into the fire, so we don't allow any of ourselves to remain in him. One of the most illuminating moments of my spiritual journey came when God revealed to me that he didn't want to destroy the Performer, Pleaser, and Protector. Instead, he wanted to integrate my human role as a branch into the fullness of the vine that is Christ. He wanted to prune back the Performer, Pleaser, and Protector so I could become a healthier branch.

UNPACKING

A few years back I had the privilege of working with a guy who'd spent most of his life perfecting the roles of Performer, Pleaser, and Protector. He'd grown up in the church, and both of his parents were in full-time ministry positions. Even though his life's ambition had more to do with music than pastoral ministry, he took advantage of the different opportunities the church offered him early in life. Before he turned 20, he was the youth pastor at his dad's church. He met the girl of his dreams on a missions trip. They fell in love, she joined him at his church, and they began to minister together. They soon married and before long were expecting their first child. His ministry was exciting, innovative, and fruitful. Students who had been far from God were coming and feeling accepted and loved. All of the outward indicators pointed to his taking over the role of senior pastor one day. He seemed to have found his ministry golden ticket.

He probably could have continued down that path for a long time, riding his father's coattails and making use of his considerable gifts. But there was a subtle but nagging hunger in his soul that was calling him to a more full and integrated life. When I met him, he didn't really have words to articulate what it was that he was hearing in his soul. But it was clear to me that he'd been living as a PPP addict for far too many years. I sensed that my friend would soon find himself sitting around the circle where his confession of addictive behavior would be listened to and received.

There was an open position at our church at the time, and he was the person I wanted to fill it. We didn't know each other that well when I called and asked him to consider leaving his comfortable position where he worked with his entire family, 80-degree winters, and a ministry he loved and had built from scratch. I was offering him a situation far from family and friends, with 15-degree January days and a brand-new ministry that needed to be built. I might have said, "No." But after many interviews and conversations, he, his wife, and their brand-new baby boy found themselves in Chicago the following July. Within weeks of his arrival, even as we were unpacking boxes filled with all his earthly belongings, we also began unpacking PPP patterns that had been developing throughout his life.

Right away he found that his old coping mechanisms were no longer working. The Performer in him wasn't getting the applause he was used to. He was in a new place and was no longer the big man on campus. The ministry he was leading was average. His flashy techniques were not well received. The people he was used to pleasing lived hundreds of miles away; he felt alone and insignificant. Freed from his long-time role as the senior pastor's firstborn son, he didn't know how to function. He was becoming more and more aware of the false selves he'd lived out of most of his life. To him it felt like his life was falling apart. But in reality, he was learning to live as his true self for the first time.

He felt powerless—yet for the first time he started feeling free. He began to realize he'd spent years polishing skills that had contributed to a false self. He ruthlessly uncovered the unhealthy trends and patterns that had become a way of life. He surrounded himself with wise people with whom he felt safe, and he invited their counsel and accountability. He took on difficult conversations with family members he'd always been afraid to disappoint. For a while, he avoided all opportunities that would feed the Performer inside him. As he kept his ears open to the questions floating through his soul, the fullness of his integrated self was being born. As he reclaimed his true nature as a branch connected to the living vine, he began to see for the first time that he was more than his accomplishments. He was more than his talents. He was more than the senior pastor's son. He was more than the Protector of his family's reputation. He was created to be wholly connected to the vine, addictions and all.

Maybe that's what God is inviting you to do as well. What if remaining in the vine looked like a PPPA meeting where we began by saying "God, I recognize that alone I am powerless over the performing, pleasing, and protecting parts of me, but I believe that you can restore me to the whole and integrated self I was created to be." Maybe we should start some meetings?

Soul School Homework

Assignment
A task to be accomplished

PPP Awareness

Spend some time rereading the definitions of the following scripts youth workers tend to learn. Be honest with yourself. Put a check mark next to the roles that you play in life.

_____ Performers look for affection and affirmation in the applause of others. They live in a continuous cycle of trying to outshine everyone else. Sometimes the Performer is called a perfectionist. The need to achieve is often the addiction that drives Performers to cover up the deep insecurities that linger within.

_____ Pleasers learn how to adapt themselves to the expectations of others. They learn what others want to hear and how they want to hear it. People love a Pleaser.

_____ Protectors spend their lives working hard to keep themselves away from any possible disappointment. They protect their feelings. They rarely take risks. They stick with what is known and what keeps them feeling safe. Often they are pessimistic about possibility and potential.

Lab
A place for practice or observation

PPP Anonymous

For years, Alcoholics Anonymous and similar 12-step groups have guided thousands of people on the journey from being addicted to a substance to becoming sober and free. The fourth step in the recovery process involves taking the time to make "a searching and fearless moral inventory" of oneself. Write out the specific ways you have been living as a Performer, Pleaser, or Protector.

Examples:

I am a *Performer*. I am driven to succeed. My decisions are almost always based on making sure someone will see the good I've done and applaud my activity. I thrive on compliments. I feel discouraged when others don't notice my skills. Here are specific ways I perform throughout my week...

I am a *Pleaser*. I want to make others happy. I base my emotions and feelings on the responses I receive from others. I work hard to please the authority figures in my life. Here are specific ways I perform throughout my week...

I am a *Protector*. I feel safest when I keep things the same. I don't like change and I am afraid of risk. Here are specific ways I protect throughout my week...

Test

A procedure for critical evaluation; a means of determining the presence, quality, or truth of something; a trial

Pruning Time

Spend some time asking God specifically where he needs to do some pruning. Is there a branch that resembles a Performer, Pleaser, or Protector that needs to be trimmed or even cut off? Meditate on this passage, asking God to prune away the PPPs in your life.

"I am the true vine, and my Father is the gardener. He cuts off every branch in me that bears no fruit, while every branch that does bear fruit he prunes so that it will be even more fruitful."

—JOHN 15:1-2

CHAPTER FIVE

Hello,

My *Real* Name Is...

Soul Lesson: Being the unique person God created you to be is one of the greatest gifts you can offer your God and this world.

BIRTHDAY

I'm sure it was quite a time for my parents. Their first child was on the way. They didn't know whether to buy a pink bonnet or blue booties. They'd hoped for a while to become parents, and now the moment was quickly approaching. The room was prepared. The appropriate baby paraphernalia had been purchased. Their lives were about to change, and mine was about to start.

My parents tell me it was a hot, sticky day in July. My mom was hoping she could hold out till the Fourth of July to have me—maybe she thought it would be easier to remember my birthday that way. But I had other plans. I was cramped for space and lacking in patience (it started at an early age), and I was ready to get the party started. My parents were surprised when the doctor said, "It's a girl!" They'd convinced themselves they were having a boy. My mom says my dad could not stop smiling, he was so excited to have a little girl; my dad says my mom could not stop crying tears of joy, since she was so overwhelmed by the moment (and I'm sure the pain added a few tears). Within a few moments of my first earthly breaths, I was given my name: Jeanne Marie. I was named after my mom's mom, Jeanne Carey, and I think they just liked the sound of Marie with it.

That's who I am. *Jeanne Marie.* I've carried that name for my entire life. It was put on my birth certificate. It sits atop every official document about me. Teachers used it to get my attention. Elementary kids created teasing rhymes with it. It's been printed on school applications and job resumes. One day someone was asked, "Do you take Jeanne Marie as your wife?" The name appeared later on another birth announcement, but this time in the section noting the mother. And this same name will one day sit on a slab of marble in a cemetery, marking July 2, 1973, as the day my life began and a dash bridging the space to the date of my death.

I like my name. I don't know too many other Jeannes. I think it fits my personality. But whenever I have to fill out one of those sticky little rectangular tags that say, "Hello, my name is...," I find myself wondering, Will people have any comprehension of who I really am when they call me by name? How could anyone possibly know the truest parts of my identity from a nametag?

I started contemplating this after I was introduced to Thomas Merton. We weren't introduced physically—he died a couple of years before I was born. But when I came upon his writing, I felt like I'd met up with a long lost friend. Thomas Merton's writings were like a spoon that stirred my brewing soul. One particular passage echoed deeply within me. Merton wrote:

> Finding that unique self is the problem on which all our existence, peace,
> and happiness depend. Nothing is more important, for if we find our true
> self we find God, and if we find God, we find our most authentic self.

I started wondering if I really knew my unique self. I knew my name. I knew my likes and dislikes. I knew whom I loved and who loved me back. I knew my abilities, my strengths and weaknesses. But who was I...really? Was my identity defined by where I lived? What I did (and how well I did it)? Did I define myself by how I looked? Did my possessions indicate who I am? Did my behavior determine my identity?

As I started to ponder these questions I felt a sense of insecurity growing in me like an out-of-control weed, eager to devour everything positive about me. I didn't like feeling insecure, so I didn't like asking these questions. I'd established many patterns over the years that seemed to "work" for me. But asking these questions was upsetting all of them. It wasn't making me feel better or closer to God. In fact, I started feeling worse. I felt like a fake. I felt confused. I felt apprehensive about who and what I was. I wanted to stop asking the questions, but the door was already open. I knew that if I walked away from the journey of discovering my true identity, I'd be walking back into a shallow and fruitless life. I had no choice but to wade into the deep waters, knowing that, even though I didn't feel better, something deep within my soul wanted to be better. I wanted to be the real me. I felt committed to finding my unique self and, more importantly, to discovering anew the one true God.

THE THREE MYTHS OF YOUTH MINISTRY IDENTITY

I've had the unique and wonderful privilege of meeting many youth workers all around the world. It is uncanny to me how often I see the same identity questions starting to flare up in the lives of different youth workers. So many of us have mastered the art of being an "artificial somebody" to the kids, parents, and churches we serve that we've lost our true selves along the way. We have each soldered a steel nameplate to our chest with some insignificant ramblings of fruitless distinction, while our true identity in Christ remains a mystery—not only to others but also to ourselves.

I have found that the places where youth workers become stuck in regard to their identities almost always fall in one or more of the following myths:

1. My identity is defined by my past.

2. My identity is defined by what I do.

3. My identity is defined by my relationships.

THE PAST

The moment you were conceived, your unique story began. Your life has been shaped by so many factors—who your parents were, when and where you were born, where you fell in the birth order, your family background, your educational experience, the friends you've made, the preferences you've developed, the pains of rejection, the joys of accomplishment, and so much more. Whatever the particulars of your past, it's likely that you developed a false identity (perhaps more than one) somewhere along the journey.

I have a close friend who was born into a situation of family distress. Her father was a Sunday-morning churchgoer who drank his way through the rest of the week. He was continually absent through most of her childhood and eventually left her mother to raise four children alone. The family lived on food stamps and found odd jobs to get by. My friend's past propelled her into a present where she has developed an identity as a survivor who does not trust men and regularly worries about whether she will have enough to get by.

I know a guy who was born into an extremely wealthy family with a lineage of Ivy League degrees and prestigious professions. He struggled through school as he hid a mild learning disability. He believed he should follow the family path into a high paying career, but his journey was complicated when he felt a call to do missionary work in a poor community. His past told him that he was nothing unless he had an influential job where he made lots of money. So he developed an identity that learned to hide his weakness and cover up his desires.

Another friend of mine was born into a family in which his parents and grandparents were all deeply entrenched in church work. My friend spent most of his childhood sitting obediently and quietly on the front pew. He went to the Christian school affiliated with his church and was protected in a bubble of fundamentalist legalism. One of his favorite escapes as a young boy was watching films, and he dreamed of being a filmmaker. His past told him Hollywood was filled with nothing but sin, and that God had crafted him for the ministry. So he let his past dictate his present. He entered the ministry and became a youth pastor, although he still quietly dreams of making films. He's learned how to play the part of a pastor, but his heart is somewhere else.

Our unique pasts affect the identities we live out of today. But our pasts do not need to be the paramount forces that define our true identities. I love the promise God declares in Isaiah:

> Forget about what's happened; don't keep going over old history. Be alert, be present. I'm about to do something brand-new. It's bursting out! Don't you see it?
>
> —ISAIAH 43:19 *(The Message)*

Clearly God does not intend that we allow our past experiences to define who we are in the present or who we will be in the future. God tells us to forget about what's happened in the past. He tells us to stop going over history, because he wants to do something new in us. I believe many of us need to hear this promise deep within our souls. What you've experienced in your past affects who you are, but it does not define who you are.

WHAT I DO

Kids are often asked, "What do you want to be when you grow up?" It is an open-ended question, yet I find it fascinating that almost every child answers in the form of a profession. I want to be a doctor. I want to be a teacher. I want to be a baseball player. I want to be a dancer. How beautiful and hysterical it would be if a six-year-old child would profess, "I want to be the unique me I was created to be—and that won't be defined by what job I do." Every adult around would faint at such an answer. Even at a young age we are conditioned to define identity by what we do. Most of us have grown up in a society that categorizes people on the basis of what they do, and how well they do it. Usually one of the first questions strangers ask each other after being introduced is "What do you do?" While there's no harm caused in asking or answering such questions, when we continually define ourselves by our work or career, we can easily come to believe that what we do determines who we are.

The difficulty of allowing ourselves to be identified solely by what we do is usually put to the test when we first face a rejection of our abilities. I remember when, as an impressionable and enthusiastic adolescent, I didn't get a part in the school play. I was devastated and deflated. I was passionate about the performing arts and had begun to identify myself as an actress. When I didn't get the affirmation of receiving the role I'd hoped for, I started wondering who I was. I began to feel insecure and rejected because I didn't have an activity that would define me.

The same experience can happen when a student works hard throughout high school only to open her mailbox one day and find a rejection letter from the university of her dreams. Or when a professional works hard at his career—going above and beyond the call, putting in extra hours in hopes of climbing the corporate ladder—then finds himself sitting in the human resources office hearing that the company is downsizing and he is out of a job.

For youth workers, the same identity issues surround many of the questions we ask one another: Where did you go to school/seminary? How big is your church? What's the size of your youth ministry? How many students are in your small group? What is your program like? How good is the worship? What kinds of events do you have? Too often we allow our youth ministry identities to be determined by what we are doing, not who we are becoming and how we are helping students become the people God intended them to be. I have looked into the tired and defeated eyes of many youth workers who feel like they can't compete or keep up with the identities they've created for themselves or those that others want them to live up to. We are on an exhausting treadmill of doing things to keep our false identities alive, while running our souls into a state of mindless and passionless doing instead of being.

I once read an interview in *Leadership Journal* in which the Christian singer, writer, and talk-show host Sheila Walsh told this story about one of the most difficult times in her own life:

In 1992 my life hit the wall. One morning I was on national television with my nice suit and my inflatable hairdo, and that night I was in the locked ward of a psychiatric hospital. It was the kindest thing God could have done for me. The very first day in the hospital, the psychiatrist asked me, "Who are you?"

"I'm the cohost of *The 700 Club*."

"That's not what I meant," he said.

"Well, I'm a writer. I'm a singer."

"That's not what I meant. Who are you?"

"I don't have a clue," I said, and he replied, "Now that's right, and that's why you're here." And the greatest thing I discovered there [was that I could be] fully known and fully loved. Jesus knew the worst, and he loved me. What a relief to know the worst about yourself and at the same moment to be embraced by God. It's so liberating to reach the end of yourself.

Sheila Walsh's story reminds us of a simple but profound truth: What we do affects who we are, but it does not define who we are.

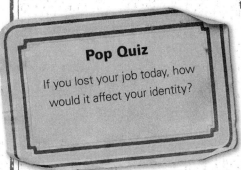

Pop Quiz

If you lost your job today, how would it affect your identity?

MY RELATIONSHIPS

Our relational worlds and status deeply affect our identity. From parents to siblings to friends to significant others to spouses to children, we're reminded throughout our lives that our relational realities play a significant role in shaping our identities.

I was talking to a good friend awhile back who decided to leave her ministry as a church youth worker to become a counselor. I asked her about her reasons for leaving her church role to go into the counseling field. She explained that she felt she would never be able to become all that God had created her to be in her church because she was a single woman. I couldn't believe that her relational status would have anything to do with her ministry in the church. But somewhere along the way she'd been told that to be an effective minister in the church she would need to be married. So she packed up her church bags and began a new career. A false identity was formed that told her that she needed to be married in order to be effective for God within church ministry.

I have another good friend whose parents split up when she was young. Her dad found a new wife and a new family, and her mom limped through life trying to keep her and her brothers together. Since my friend was the oldest child, she picked up the slack of taking care of her brothers. She took on a parental role in her household because her father was absent and her mother unstable. At a young age a false identity was being formed that told her she needed to be taking care of someone else in order to be significant. She always puts her desires and dreams on the shelf to tend to the needs of others.

I know a guy who cannot be alone. He's found a way to move from one romantic relationship to another without ever being single. He loves the safety he feels while in a dating relationship, but he hates the thought of a marriage commitment. So whenever a dating relationship gets too serious, he breaks it off and quickly starts up a new relationship. Over the years he's formed a false identity rooted in fears of being alone and of making a commitment, so he's learned to function as the perpetual bachelor.

The specific experiences of our relational worlds deeply affect how we see ourselves. Our relational realities often dictate how we function in the world—and sometimes even give us names. If your marriage has fallen apart, then your relational identity labels you a divorced person. If you've lost your parents, then your relational identity labels you an orphan. If you cannot have children, then your relational identity labels you infertile. If you've suffered emotional, physical, or sexual abuse from a family member or someone else, then your relational identity labels you abused. If you've lost a spouse, then your relational identity labels you a widow or widower...

Our relationships play such a large role in the growth of our identities. Many of us have suffered deep pains in our relational experiences. Often the power and intensity of these experiences begin to form identities within us that stray far from our original design. And the way we see ourselves relationally, as well as the way others experience us relationally, affects how we live. Any time we allow our relational realities to alter the truth of who we are, we do damage to our most essential and beautiful relational identity: Each of us is a beloved child of God. We have a true identity that extends beyond our earthly relational experiences. No matter what we may encounter, we can rest secure that our status as God's children will never change.

"How great is the love the Father has lavished on us, that we should be called children of God! And that is what we are!" (1 John 3:1). We *are* God's children, we always *have been* his children, and we always *will be* his children. This is the essential relational truth that defines our lives. Your other relational realities affect who you are, but they do not determine who you are.

DISCOVERING ONE'S TRUE NAME

As my identity road trip has continued over the years, I've realized my true identity is not defined by my past or what I do or my relational status. Sometimes I lose my way and make a U-turn that sends me back down the same false identity roads I've traveled before. But I've done some serious wrestling in an effort to begin to see myself for who I really am, and share the gift of my true self with others.

It's certainly not possible for any of us to simply put on a nametag that says, "Hello, my name is..." and have others instantly know the truth of who we are. But I believe that God has placed something unique within each one of us, a word God wants to speak into the world through our lives. As Thomas Merton once wrote:

> God utters me like a word containing a partial thought of himself. A word
> will never be able to comprehend the voice that utters it. But, if I am true

to the concept God utters in me, if I am true to the thought in him I was meant to embody, I shall be full of his actuality and find him everywhere in myself, and find myself nowhere. I shall be lost in him.

Pop Quiz

Do you let your relationships define who you are?

I had an experience while leading a student ministry staff team awhile back that radically ingrained Merton's words into my identity. Every other quarter the members of our team would go away together for a few days for the purpose of relational and spiritual connection with one another. On one such retreat, I decided to use Merton's quote as a guiding theme for our time together. What emerged from our conversation was a moving experience in which, one by one, we sent each member of our team out of the room, while the rest of the community came up with a word or a phrase that we sensed God was trying to utter through that person's life. We then brought the person back into the room, sat them in the middle of the circle, and showered them with encouragement and affirmation about their true identity and how we saw aspects of God through their lives. We then gave each person a canvas with Thomas Merton's quote and a new name written on it. I still remember some of the names given:

April is strong, consistent, and able to illuminate truth. We told her she reminds us of God's guidance in our lives and how he brings light to dark situations. We gave her the name Pillar of Fire.

Josh is an inspiring leader full of fresh ideas. We told him that he reminds us of how God is about making all things new and is an imaginative Creator. We gave him the name New Wineskins.

Craig is brilliantly gifted in diverse ways, and is also one of the most faithful people I know. We told him he reminds us of God's love and dynamic devotion to all people. We gave him the name Intricately Devoted.

Rebecca fills up a room with her energy, humor, and magnetic personality. She's a constant reminder of God's powerful presence and joy. For her name, we actually made up a word. We gave her the name Charasmagnetic.

Eric is one of the most authentic people I know. You always know what he's thinking. We told him he reminds us of God's truth and pure love. We gave him the name Unedited Authenticity.

Jesse is one of those people who's always brewing with a new idea about how to express God's love to others. We told him he reminds us of God's kindness and creativity. We gave him the name Tender Brilliance.

The names given to these unique children of God had nothing to do with their pasts, their jobs, or their relational status. But they had everything to do with the unique way in which God's character was spoken in their lives, the unique person God created each of them to be. Maybe when Jesus told Simon that, from here on out, his name was going to be Peter (which means *rock*), he was reminding Peter of the unique way God wanted to reveal his love for the church through Peter's life. Perhaps when Jesus told James and John that they were going to be known as the Sons of Thunder, he was naming the unique ways God's power would echo through their lives.

Genesis 1:27 reminds us that every one of us carries the likeness of God: "So God created human beings in his own image, in the image of God he created them; male and female he created them." We are made in the image of God. We are like him. He is our master blueprint. He is the pattern from which each of us is cut. So every person's life and identity must have something in it that reveals the Divine identity.

We need to reclaim our real identity as children of God. We need to embrace ourselves for who we really are and allow God to melt our false nametags and write on us our true names. So the next time you have to fill out a nametag, maybe you need to ask yourself what it is that God is trying to reveal in your life. Maybe that will point to what your real name is...as far as God is concerned.

Soul School Homework

Assignment
A task to be accomplished

Myth Buster

Many of us struggle with myths that our identity is defined by one of the following areas.

My identity is defined by my past.

My identity is defined by what I do.

My identity is defined by my relationships.

Spend some time considering the following questions to see if you need to bust any of these myths in your own life. If you answer "Yes" or "Sometimes" to any of the questions, spend some time contemplating how you might need to bust that identity myth.

MY PAST

1. There are experiences in my past that I continue to play out in my mind.

    YES   NO   SOMETIMES

2. There are experiences in my past that contribute to how I interact with others.

    YES   NO   SOMETIMES

3. There are experiences in my past that I've not healed and they affect who I am today.

    YES   NO   SOMETIMES

MY WORK

4. I find a lot of my worth in what I do.

    YES   NO   SOMETIMES

5. I spend too much time and emotional energy making sure I do my job well.

   YES   NO   SOMETIMES

6. One of the first questions I ask people is "What do you do?"

   YES   NO   SOMETIMES

MY RELATIONSHPS

7. It is important to me who I know.

   YES   NO   SOMETIMES

8. It is important to me that people know about my relational status—married, single, parent, dating, etc.

   YES   NO   SOMETIMES

9. I am discontented with my relational world. I regularly seem to find myself in broken relationships.

   YES   NO   SOMETIMES

Lab
A place for practice or observation

Uniquely Me

Spend some time listing those things that make you unique—talents, skills, experiences, characteristics, relationships, etc. Be as comprehensive as you can, and try not to leave anything out. You may even want to ask someone else to look at the list and contribute to the inventory of what makes you "you." Consider how these particularities might contribute to the unique truth God seeks to reveal through you.

Test

A procedure for critical evaluation; a means of determining the presence, quality, or truth of something; a trial

New Name

Take the list you've created in the lab section and try to boil it down to a word or a phrase that embodies what God might be trying to say in your life. Ask others to help you determine how they see God's character in you, and then write down the name or phrase you sense God speaking in your life.

God utters me like a word containing a partial thought of himself. A word will never be able to comprehend the voice that utters it. But, if I am true to the concept God utters in me, if I am true to the thought in him I was meant to embody, I shall be full of his actuality and find him everywhere in myself, and find myself nowhere. I shall be lost in him.

—THOMAS MERTON

CHAPTER SIX

The Miraculous Middle

Soul Lesson: As we learn to embrace what is broken within us, we become miraculously whole and better able to reflect the love and beauty of Christ.

THEOLOGIAN? NO; YOUTH WORKER? YES!

Soul School is a journey. It is the journey God invited me to go on, and I believe to the core of my being that it's a journey God invites every one of his children to join. That's why I'm writing this book. I am not writing *Soul School* because the book-stores of our world need one more title to sell. I'm not writing it because God needs me to send out his invitations to the Soul School party—last time I checked, his own delivery system was doing fine. And I'm certainly not writing because I'm a brilliant theologian. I'm a youth pastor who has been in the trenches. I'm writing because I want to prod and encourage others who sense, as I did, that their stories are moving toward enrollment in the School of the Soul.

One of the most marvelous lessons I continue to learn in this ongoing journey concerns the mysterious way God redeems and restores what is broken and bruised within each of us. As I started to live from my true identity, I realized I'd sometimes been a master at camouflaging what was really going on in my life. At times I've lived more in hiding than in the freedom that comes from being open and vulnerable. And as I've looked around at the others in the field of youth ministry, I've sensed that many of them are proficient in the same art. One of humanity's greatest magic tricks is that we've learned to cover our flaws and lost the ability to authentically admit our flaws and injuries. For too long, I thought God's desire was that I dig out all of my junk and try to throw it away through my own human efforts. But I've realized that what God really wants is for me to actually embrace my humanity and become aware and honest about my brokenness and sinfulness so that I could then live from a place of authentic deep need for Jesus. Being honest about our own brokenness and sin ultimately places us in a posture of dependence on a Savior. But the beauty of our Redeemer is that we are invited to stand dependent without a life sentence demanding that we remain damaged.

It was confusing to me to embrace the parts of myself that I had always felt should be rejected. My understanding had always been that brokenness was just bad, and my job was to rid my life of it. But this simplistic understanding lacks the beauty and mystery of who Jesus is as Messiah. Jesus longs to free us from sin, but he does not reject our broken and sinful beings. In fact, he radically embraces the very aspects of us that cause many of us to live in shame.

HACK ACCOUNTABILITY

Anyone who has been in or around ministry for long has probably heard a message or two on the importance of confessing sin. Many of us have been challenged by the call to live out our faith within a loving community of accountability partners. The freedom that comes from doing life with other believers is liberating. But I've found that the level of liberation I experience is directly related to the level of authenticity with which I am willing to live.

In my ministry I've served as a leader or participant in many different kinds of small groups—from book studies to prayer groups to hard-core accountability partnerships. I have been under the loving care of a spiritual director, and I've also played the role of spiritual director in many different lives. In that time, I've heard just about every different kind of sin confessed—and I've confessed a lot of them myself. I think confession is very important. But I think many of us mistakenly think that once our sin is out of the bag, then we're in the clear. Since we've already cast the spotlight on our fallen humanity, we think we can just give a "ditto" to the sin we confessed last time our group met. I don't think this really helps us live in the light. Maybe the initial exposure brings some relief, but it's just like diagnosing a sickness. We can acknowledge that our symptoms are a runny nose, a cough, and a high temperature, but until we recognize the virus lingering beneath the symptoms, there is little hope of healing.

I used to be part of a small group that held its weekly meetings at 5:30 a.m. I can't remember who decided it would be a good idea for us to meet that early, but once a week we got up before the sun and gathered for breakfast, prayer, and Bible study. We loved being together, and I'm sure that's one reason we were able to pull ourselves from the comfort of our warm beds to spend time with one another. The group was an unusual assemblage of people—but we had great chemistry and there was a general feeling of trust and safety among the group. We were all in a similar stage of life, but each of us was facing distinct challenges. We'd been together as a group for only a few months when one group member took a risk that forever changed the way we would interact with one another.

During a routine time of catching up with one another, this person courageously opened up. "I am really struggling with something I feel embarrassed to share," she said, "but I know I need to bring this into the light. I struggle with an occasional stretching of the truth." I think every one of us was impressed with the honesty and spirit in which my friend shared, and we all nodded our heads as a sign of encouragement and affirmation and perhaps even a silent confession that each of us had been known to stretch the truth. But in the moments that followed, I experienced a new level of vulnerability and humility in confession. She continued: "I lie because I wonder if people would accept me if they knew who I really was. So instead of being authentic, I make up stories. I lie about things that have happened. In fact, there are parts of my life that are a complete fabrication. I think, at the core of who I am, I wonder if I'm worthy of being loved. There are so many things in my past that I'm ashamed of. I can't imagine there is enough grace for someone like me. So I've become a master at making my life look much better than it really is."

I'm sure the silence that followed her confession must have felt like an eternity for my friend, until another member of the group began to speak: "I struggle with anger, and it causes me to lose my temper sometimes. I've spent a number of years being angry. I constantly feel like God is out to get me. Everything seems to go wrong in my life. I'm just not sure whether I really believe that God is good. So the only way I can retaliate is to get angry with God, but I end up taking it out on the people who are most important to me. My anger has led me on a downward spiral of rage, bitterness, and resentment."

Then another member of the group spoke up: "I struggle with lust, and it has caused me to dabble in pornography. I'm afraid my sexual needs won't ever be met. Somewhere inside I guess I wonder whether God is enough for me, because I keep looking to others to give me temporary fulfillment."

Each member of the group followed suit, lovingly sharing their own personal sins or failures. But what happened that morning was more than confession. We didn't just admit that we'd struggled with anger, lies, or lust. There was a spirit of determination to get to the root of our distinct sin. We searched our own hearts seeking an honest diagnosis for how the sin had taken root in our lives. We dug into one another's stories. We asked questions. We challenged one another to go deeper. We began to embrace one another's stories, and we started to live in the dark and light of our lives.

Confession is a strange thing. Some people seem to have become overly comfortable with their own stories of sin and brokenness and wounds. At times our stories can be overly magnified, telling everyone we meet: *I'm a sinner. I am broken. I'm messed up. Broken. Bruised. This is who I am—nothing more, nothing less. Take it or leave it.* I have seen youth workers inappropriately use the particular sins of their own lives as a ministry tool to try to relate to their students. They are nonchalant about their depravity, seeming almost haphazard in divulging their sins as a way to identify with students who are struggling. Others minimize their sin, focusing only on the fact that they are forgiven. These folks seem to forget the price that was paid so they could claim their identity as blameless and clean. They live without an appropriate gratitude and dependency on Jesus. These youth workers are easy to detect because of the halos they've placed above their own heads and their false personas of perfection and pride. Whenever we magnify our sin and act as if it represents all that we are, or when we minimize the incredible price Jesus paid so our sin could be forgiven, we miss the incredible mystery and paradox of the Christian life: *In Christ we can be both broken and whole at the same time.*

MIRACULOUS PARADOX

I wish I completely understood how God could be both entirely just and entirely merciful at the same time. It is mind-bending that God's justice is not bigger than his mercy, nor is his mercy bigger than his justice. In fact, God's justice and mercy gloriously complement and depend on each other. We cannot experience or understand the breadth of God's mercy without experiencing and understanding the breadth of his justice. And the reverse is equally true; we cannot experience or understand the totality of his justice without experiencing and understanding the totality of his mercy. The two coexist beautifully without canceling each other out.

Maybe this is similar to how God longs for us to live with regard to our own wholeness and brokenness. My brokenness is incomplete unless I recognize that God wants to put me in a place of wholeness. My wholeness means nothing unless I recognize the price paid to make me whole. So the miraculous middle is in embracing that I am broken, but at the same time, I have been made whole. When I started to understand this in my life, bells of liberation began to sound for the first time. By embracing myself as a complex paradox, a both/and being, I started to live in the truth that I am both broken and miraculously whole.

STITCHES, SLINGS, & SCARS

While I was growing up, my family seemed to have a regular room reserved at our local ER. It's not that my brothers and I were clumsy and prone to accidents, it's that we were risky and often stupid and prone to accidents. There have been many Thanksgiving meals when we have recounted the stories of old when each of us went to the hospital for our stupid human tricks. Many of our visits sent us home with casts, stitches, slings, and crutches. After our breaks, wounds, and cuts healed, we were often left with "battle scars." For example, there was the time after a big snowfall when I went sledding down a neighbor's driveway on a garbage can lid. The seven stitches I received and the scar on my chin serve as reminders to consider a sled instead of a garbage can lid the next time I go sledding. Or the time when we were discovering the power of gravity by throwing some of my dad's tools up in the air to see where they would land. Gravity was not kind to my brother Eddie, as one hammer landed right on his head, causing a scar that's now hidden beneath his hair. Then there was the time we were playing "King of the Mountain" on a large mound of dirt in the neighborhood. I informed my brother Andy that I was the "Queen of the Mountain" and if he came to the top I would physically communicate to him my superior role by hitting him with my shovel. Despite many kind reminders, he decided to not heed my warning, and he now has a scar on his forehead that reminds him that—for a day—I was queen of the mountain. And I, in turn, received a punishment that reminded me for the rest of the summer that I would not be handling a shovel again.

> The Lord is compassionate and gracious, slow to anger, abounding in love. He will not always accuse, nor will he harbor his anger forever; he does not treat us as our sins deserve or repay us according to our iniquities. For as high as the heavens are above the earth, so great is his love for those who fear him; as far as the east is from the west, so far has he removed our transgressions from us.
>
> —PSALM 103:8–12

Just as my brothers and I have little scars that remind us of past mistakes, we all have war wounds of sin and brokenness that tell of our capacity to stray and our destitution without a Savior. Yet the amazing mystery is that God not only forgives our sins, he blots them from our permanent record. God walks us into a place of healing. Even if we can see our own spiritual scars, God forgets they've ever existed.

God does not see us as limping, scarred, wounded, or damaged—and he longs for us to see ourselves as he sees us. He has cleaned us up and called us to live as free, transformed, new creations. The power and possibilities that stem from such radical forgiveness still drop me to my knees. I pray that I will remain in such a posture of dependency for the rest of my life.

One of the greatest joys of working in youth ministry is that I get a front-row seat to seeing this kind of metamorphosis in the lives of students, leaders, parents, and staff. As I was working on this chapter, I thought of a friend and former teammate that I'd been able to walk with as he journeyed through the paradox of being both broken and whole simultaneously. I asked him to read a rough draft of the chapter, which led us into a long conversation about the mystery unleashed in our lives when we live in this incredible paradox. Later he sent me an excerpt from his journal in which he reflected on the way that mystery has shaped his own spiritual journey. I thought you would appreciate his story:

Met Jeanne tonight to discuss her book. Our conversation reminded me of the biggest lesson I've had to learn over the past 13 years: that I, too, am sometimes a flop, a sinner, bruised by life, needy—an emotional, relational and spiritual mess. I constantly need God for forgiveness, healing and endurance. And I need to remind myself of my dependence on him, lest I become a prideful little brat.

These truths first assaulted "invincible" me when I got ensnared in sexual sin and drug use, grappling with remorse. I faced them again during my first year in ministry; in the midst of a church-wide conflict, I found myself no better than the corruption around me: willing to lie, act arrogantly toward my superiors, and harbor unhealthy resentment. It's been an even bigger struggle to embrace wounds dealt to me from others—my family, friends who've disappeared, girlfriends who've dumped me. In avoiding "victim" mentality, I've cheated myself of legitimate grief, of having a chance to rest with Jesus in my pain.

*I don't dare underestimate the value of these lessons—or deny that I'm given opportunities to relearn dependence daily. But when I first met Jeanne, I think my wounds had morphed into festering open sores. Every message I gave meandered its way 'round to confession time, during which high schoolers contemplating making out were instead invited to inspect their souls for junk to bring to Jesus. Every one-on-one with a troubled student descended into a recounting of **my own** struggles. The intention was to let students know they were not alone; in reality, they left my office either cheered that they were less of a wreck than I was or distressed at my insufficiency as a role model. My bookshelf told the whole story: **The Wounded Healer, The Raga-***

*muffin Gospel, **The Dark Night of the Soul**—wonderful and wise books that I took to their bleakest extremes.*

*And this is how I remember Jeanne dealing with me (in matching two-piece track suit with megaphone): "Hey! Those are things you've done and that've been done to you, but **that's not who you are now!** Don't stop short by just embracing the brokenness and woundedness that's part of your story; extend **even more love** to the forgiven, healed, and whole person Jesus has redeemed from the wreckage. Lead not only out of humility, dependence, and awareness of your frailty, **but** also out of the power, strength and endurance imparted to you by God."*

*And she was right. (There it is, in print.) Along the way I'd decided that, each time God did business with me, he arrested whatever behaviors, hurts, and sins existed in my life, loosening their future grip. But I didn't sense that his work was also retroactive—miraculously expunging whatever came before and providing me a new identity. Instead of counseling with "I've succumbed to sexual temptation and must rely on God's grace to get through every day," I could claim "I'm a virgin and temptation has no power over me!" No more "I'm prone to enmeshment with my mother because I'm a Pleaser." Rather, I could don the mantle of an independent young man, appropriately dutiful **and** able to set boundaries. So much of what Jeanne encouraged me to profess seemed like fantastical thinking, but as I lived into this new skin, I found endless promises that I'd not yet claimed. And I watched myself living from an identity still rooted in God—but focused on his unbelievable work rather than my persistent need.*

*Of course, both sides of the equation are true: I am dependent **and** wildly powerful. I can't quite get my arms around that. But I'm pretty sure I wouldn't have seen the complexity and the mystery unless Jeanne had challenged me.*

The wonder and awe of the miraculous middle has not worn off in my life. I am still amazed that in Jesus we can be both broken and whole. We are far more than just the sum of what we've done or what's been done to us. Each of us is simultaneously both broken and complete. The experience of this perplexing reality in my own life keeps me in a posture of profound gratitude and dependence. I am grateful that I've been able to experience this mystery myself and walk with others in their own journeys.

Soul School Homework

Assignment
A task to be accomplished

These Are a Few of Our Favorite Sins

Here are some common sins I've seen in the lives of youth workers. Spend some time working through this list. Circle those sins that you struggle with on a regular basis.

Arrogance—A spirit of superiority, self-importance, and pride.

Gossip—Speaking about others behind their backs.

Image—Always concerned with how you appear to others.

Judgmentalism—Looking at the flaws of others before looking at your own.

Lying—Not communicating the truth.

Pornography—Viewing inappropriate images of others.

Rage—Intense unprocessed anger.

Rebellion—Resistance or defiance of authority.

Recognition—The unhealthy need to be affirmed or acknowledged for your actions.

Resentment—Holding on to bitterness or anger.

Sexual Sin—Engaging in inappropriate sexual activity.

Spiritual Neglect—Letting ministry activity replace your spiritual life.

Use the space below to write any other sins with which you struggle that may not have been mentioned.

Lab
A place for practice or observation

Clean Up

Meditate on the passage below. Ask God to cleanse your life. Confess the sins that you've acknowledged above and confess them aloud to God. Ask him to renew you and restore you to joy and wholeness.

> Create in me a pure heart, O God, and renew a steadfast spirit within me. Do not cast me from your presence or take your Holy Spirit from me. Restore to me the joy of your salvation and grant me a willing spirit, to sustain me. Then I will teach transgressors your ways, and sinners will turn back to you.
>
> **—PSALM 51:10-13**

Test

A procedure for critical evaluation; a means of determining the presence, quality, or truth of something; a trial

Embracing the Paradox

Spend some time allowing the miraculous paradox of being both broken and whole to bring you hope and healing. For each of the sins you've acknowledged, write out a statement similar to the examples below. Allow the truth of the statement to bring you into the miraculous middle of being both broken and whole.

Examples:

I am a sinner. I confess that I spiritually neglect my relationship with you, God. I embrace that this sin causes me to be broken, but because of Jesus I can be made whole.

I am a sinner. I confess that I am obsessed with receiving recognition. I embrace that this sin causes me to be broken, but because of Jesus I can be made whole.

SECTION THREE

Reaching Out

My 16-month-old son, Elijah, is learning new words every day. He's quickly gone from getting by with a few staples like "please" and "milk" to a stage where he's repeating almost everything he hears. I love to watch him as he tries to put together how to say a word and contemplates what it means. My husband and I decided to take advantage of his impressionable mind to teach him that he is on a team. So we will ask him, "Elijah, who is on your team?" In his adorable high-pitched squeaky voice, he will name each member of our immediate family: "Mommy, Daddy, Li-jees (his phonetic version of his own name), and Molly (our 75-pound emotionally needy yellow Labrador retriever, who happens to be Elijah's favorite member of the team)." At 16 months Elijah knows he is a member of a little team. He knows he's part of the little community known as the Stevens family.

Elijah does not know the word *belong* yet, but he has experienced what it means. When Jarrett and I walk into his room in the morning, Elijah knows that his team has come to take care of him. When he sees us coming down the hall at church, he knows he is the only little boy we are there for. When he falls and hurts himself, he knows one of his team members will be there to swoop him up and kiss his wounds. Because of Elijah's limited vocabulary, he could not describe what community is and how important it is for each of us to have that sense of belonging—but he knows how it works, because he belongs to a team.

> The future of the church depends on whether it develops true community. We can get by for a while on size, skilled communication, and programs to meet every need, but unless we sense that we belong to each other, with masks off, the vibrant church of today will become the powerless church of tomorrow. Stale, irrelevant, a place of pretense where sufferers suffer alone, where pressure generates conformity rather than the Spirit creating life—that's where the church is headed unless it focuses on community.
>
> **—LARRY CRABB, FROM HIS FOREWORD TO *THE CONNECTING CHURCH* BY RANDY FRAZEE**

We all want to belong. We want to be part of something. We want to be accepted and loved by others regardless of our gifts and limitations. Even though belonging is a universal desire within every human heart, most people live without true community. In a world that has become obsessed with "ME," far too many people exist in loneliness and isolation. We are self-centered, self-obsessed, and self-consumed. We focus on being individuals instead of community members who belong to one another. But to be healthy individuals, we need supportive communities that reflect back to us who we really are and help us grow into the people God calls us to be.

It is in community that we can truly experience the freedom that comes from being accepted and loved. Community puts skin on loving others as ourselves and receiving that same love. We taste forgiveness, we learn how to submit, we share life, and we invite others to join us as coauthors of our personal stories.

The greatest moments of my life are always better when shared with others, and my deepest moments of pain find comfort in community. We need to let people in. We need to make ourselves vulnerable, to take off our masks so others can see who we really are. Doing life in the context of community is the only way we will stay enrolled in the School of the Soul.

CHAPTER SEVEN

The Freedom of Forgiveness

Soul Lesson: An authentic posture of humility is required in both confessing our wrongs and offering forgiveness.

CLAUSTROPHOBIC CONDITION

I'd never struggled with claustrophobia before. But as the three of us sat together in the very small yet significant space, I felt as if all the oxygen had been pressed out of the room. I felt horribly uncomfortable. I could hardly breathe. I'd have given anything to be somewhere else.

The agenda for the meeting had only one item on it: *Forgiveness.* The last thing I wanted to do was utter the phrase, "I'm sorry." By holding on to those 2½ little yet extremely powerful words, I felt I could remain in control. To apologize was to admit defeat, and I thought I was right and my boss was in the wrong. We'd gotten ourselves into such a deep mess of disagreement and dysfunction that we couldn't dig out of it by ourselves, so we asked for the assistance of a wise mediator. As the three of us sat in that tiny room, I had lots of contradictory emotions swimming within me. I was angry with him, and I'd arrogantly determined he was the guilty party and I was the innocent victim. I stubbornly believed I had nothing to apologize for. I felt embarrassed that we'd had to turn to our church leaders for help in resolving our issues. I felt misunderstood and unfairly labeled. Yet somehow I was reluctantly hopeful that God could still help us find a healthy way to move forward—and that's the only thing that caused me to show up.

The conversations that took place in that sacred space over many weeks are a living reminder to me that God is exceedingly more powerful and capable than my expectations. I'd been convinced neither of us would ever own our junk and humbly apologize and seek forgiveness. But through lots of prayer, vulnerability, tears, and surrendering of our wills, we experienced what felt like a miracle. Each of us began to see the other side of the story. The contempt I'd felt was gradually replaced with compassion. The pride that had burrowed into my heart was somehow transformed into humility. I realized I needed to ask for forgiveness. I was not just a victim. I'd made intentional choices that I needed to own and apologize for. As my boss and I allowed ourselves to be humbled, our hearts softened to a place of even wanting to forgive. Somehow over time each of us was able to tenderly utter the words, "I'm sorry. I was wrong. Will you forgive me?" And we were both able to extend forgiveness to each other.

IS BEING RIGHT REALLY BETTER THAN BEING WRONG?

I've never met anyone whose stated ambition in life is to fail, make mistakes, hurt people, and fumble royally as much as possible. (Maybe you know someone who seems to live as if this is his or her life's mission, but you should probably keep that name to yourself!) Most people want to be right, free from mistakes, and as close to perfect as possible. And too many of us, if we realize we are in error, will seek a way to cover it up. Unfortunately, this is especially true among people in leadership positions. We very rarely see public people in authoritative positions uttering the words, "I'm sorry. I was wrong. Will you forgive me?" The dominant thinking among most leaders is "Being right is always better than being wrong."

I was enrolled in that same school of thought at one time. I'm the firstborn in my family. I have a dominant personality, and I was raised in a healthy household where I was encouraged to state my opinion—and I did. As I began to develop as a young leader, the church leaders I looked to didn't offer many examples of how to live humbly in a posture of weakness while admitting their wrongs. Most of the church leaders I watched were hell-bent on being right and force-ful in their condemnation of who and what was wrong. So I started down the same path. As a young youth worker, I rarely admitted my mistakes. I was ambitious about gain-ing more authority. I was often harsh when I pointed out errors in others. I'd become judgmental and was travel-ing down a road toward life as a Pharisee. Having the rug pulled out from underneath me was the greatest thing that could have happened, because it forced me to stare into the mirror and see my own pride and arrogance. As I sat in that room with my boss and another church leader and lived in the mess I'd helped create, I finally came to a place of authentic humility and excruciating dependence. Being wrong and owning it at a core level for the first time was very, very right! I wanted that horrible uncomfortable period of my life to be over after about 5 seconds, but God was not interested in my opinion on the timing.

That season of my life lasted more than three years—with frequent, ongoing return visits. One change that came from my time in that dark cocoon of transforma-tion was a commitment to make sure I regularly uttered the words, "I'm sorry. I was wrong. Will you forgive me?" I wrote them on a piece of paper and put it above my desk. I wanted those words in my face daily. I realized something was very wrong with me if I reached the end of my week without ever uttering those words.

I was surprised by what happened to me as I began to embrace my capacity for being wrong. I started seeing that I was wrong a lot more than I'd ever realized. And when I actually started to embrace my failures rather than trying to cover them up, it gave me many opportunities to learn. Being wrong was causing me to grow much more than being right ever did.

I have a good friend whom I admire greatly. She is an incredible leader, an in-sightful mother, and an inspiring communicator. She once told me about the day she dropped her first daughter off at college. My friend handed her highly achieving child a journal and told her to end each day by writing out three mistakes she'd made that day. She encouraged her daughter to make mistakes that "counted" because, after all, they were going in writing. She told her to put her "mistake journal" under her pillow each night as a reminder that, even though she didn't do everything right, the earth was still spinning, God was still God, the sun would appear tomorrow, and she'd have another opportunity to grow.

I know lots of youth workers who need to go out and buy mistake journals. (I also know lots of pastors who need them, but that's not what this book is about.) The potential that waits within our failures when we are willing to admit them and seek forgiveness from one another is some of the best spiritual formation available. Too many of us are sending blaring signals to the next generation of leaders that being stubborn, arrogant, and argumentative and holding a grudge are telltale signs of a leader. We need to be the ones to turn the tide and offer a new picture.

DO NOT BE AFRAID

One reason so many of us have such a hard time acknowledging our wrongs and seeking forgiveness is that we're afraid. We're afraid of admitting defeat. We're afraid of consequences. We're afraid of being found out. Our pride has been in control for so long that we fear what it would look like if we really humbled ourselves and sought forgiveness when we were wrong. We're afraid of feeling out of control. Fear is also a primary reason that many of us struggle to offer forgiveness when we have been wronged. We're afraid of having to give up our grudges—many of us are more comfortable holding on to the pain of the past than being released to a freedom that's possible in the present. We're afraid of appearing weak. Fear is a debilitating disease that the Enemy knows can handicap any leader. Fear almost always stands in the way of forgiveness—whether we need to ask for it or offer it. Our only hope of escaping fear is love.

> There is no fear in love. But perfect love drives out fear, because fear has
> to do with punishment. The one who fears is not made perfect in love.
>
> —1 JOHN 4:18

As I read through the Bible, I am amazed at how often God tells his people, "Do not be afraid" or "Fear not." The One who created us knows we have a deep propensity to be afraid. Our humanity, when it is not consumed with God's love, has a tendency to drift toward fear. Many of us camouflage our fear so that, at first glance, our behavior probably doesn't look fearful at all. Many of us cover up fear with control. We become stubborn in order to protect ourselves. Or we step into a posture of pride and arrogance. We start responding to others with argumentative tones and holding grudges, hoping this will keep us feeling protected and powerful. When faced with conflict, division, or brokenness in a relationship, many of us try to bolster our strength so we appear dominant and in control. But internally we are afraid. If we just stop all our efforts to cover it up, the layers of fear that lie beneath start to float to the surface.

WINDS OF LOVE

I met my best friend Ami my freshman year of college. Our friendship was birthed as we discovered our common love of leaving class early to catch the last sunrays of the day, long conversations in quaint coffee shops, shopping for the perfect bargain, and eating out at fabulous restaurants. Over the years Ami has been with me through some of my deepest belly-aching laughter as well as some of my hardest heaving cries. Our relationship has included tastes of the greatest joys of life and the deepest pains of death. When I first met Ami, she'd just lost her mother to a painful, life-stealing disease. She was deep in the throes of grief and pain. She'd always been close to her mom and was struggling to figure out how she was going to navigate life without her. Ami was also very close to her dad, but he was also grieving and dealing with the loss of his wife. Ami struggled over the decision to go back to school after her mom's death, but her dad encouraged her to keep moving on with her life.

While Ami was away at school, she learned that her father had started a relationship with another woman in their church. Perhaps it was a way he was working through his own pain. Only a few short months after the death of her mother, Ami's father announced that he was getting married, and he asked that the family be happy and supportive of his new relationship. Ami was in knots over her dad's decision. Her own healthy process of walking through pain and grief was being hijacked by her dad's desire for her to feel joy and excitement over his new wife. Ami had no idea how to support her dad authentically, and their close bond started to suffer. Her relationship with her new stepmother was filled with forced smiles and awkward conversations. Her stepmom was cold, distant, and harsh toward Ami, which made the family dynamics even more difficult.

For many years and through many ups and downs, Ami battled the breakdown in the relationship with her dad. During a season of some honest conversation and healthy momentum toward a renewed connection with her dad, Ami got a phone call that her dad had suffered a heart attack while on vacation with his new wife. She instantly flew to the Bahamas to be with him. She was told his odds of surviving were very small, and that he should be flown back to the States. So Ami, her stepmom, and her father (who was in a coma) flew back home. Ami and her family soon recognized her father was not going to live, so they said their good byes—and Ami walked into a new life as a young woman in her 20s without either parent.

The second Ami called me, I jumped in the car to be with her, since I knew the process of burying her father was going to be incredibly difficult. In the months and years that followed, the loss of both parents and the ongoing difficult relationship with her stepmom was an emotional roller coaster that carried Ami from anger to rage to bitterness to confusion to deep sadness—with many other stops along the way. The depth of Ami's loss was affecting every area of her life. Her marriage, her children, her other family relationships, her work, and her friendships all felt the impact. The pain grew even more exaggerated as the relationship with her stepmom became increasingly more difficult. I watched Ami battle through her anger for the better part of two years. We talked regularly, processing her grief, loss, and new reality of being orphaned. But I watched my dear friend live in the angst and torment of holding so much anger and bitterness within. She had unresolved anger toward her dad. She was angry about how poorly her stepmom had treated her throughout the past few years. Ami was bursting with a venom that was debilitating her life, but she was afraid to let it go. She didn't want to release her anger because she felt that would justify what had gone on in her relationship with both her dad and her stepmom. Her anger had become a way of living, and facing that anger would require great courage, and even greater love. She felt she'd been wronged and could not figure out how to move on.

Pop Quiz

Is fear preventing you from offering forgiveness to someone or from asking forgiveness for something you've done?

I had planned a trip out to visit her. Before my visit we talked about her desire to move to a place of freedom. She was tired of living with so much bound-up pain. So after I arrived, we went up to the mountains and spent the day with God. In the morning Ami and I each spent some time alone. I'd written out a few questions for her to journal about to help get to the bottom of her hurt. *What do you most want to say to God? What are you most angry about with your stepmom? What is standing in the way of you offering forgiveness?* Ami spent the morning journaling, and I spent the time praying that God would somehow break through.

We met up for lunch, then made our way to a rose garden to process our mornings. As we sat and talked, I kept feeling this burning sense that I should ask Ami if she was ready to forgive. I finally gave in to the constant nudge (which I am confident was the Holy Spirit), and came right out and said, "You have to forgive if you ever want to be free again." Through tears Ami agreed. So we bowed our heads together, and I walked Ami through a prayer time of forgiveness. First, Ami focused on the areas where she'd made mistakes and needed to ask for forgiveness. She humbled herself and looked at her own flaws. Then, she named the offenses that had caused her pain. She placed those burdens in the hands of Jesus, and she released her anger.

As we prayed through her anger toward specific family members, we walked through moment after moment where Ami had been deeply wounded. Finally, we reached a time when Ami felt ready to say, "God, through your strength and by your grace, I forgive my dad and stepmom." As she said those words, a gust of wind swept through the rose garden. The wind was loud, strong, and sudden—before that moment, I hadn't felt even a flutter of moving air all day. That breeze lasted for a few minutes and then was gone. Ami and I both stopped—overcome by the presence of God and the way he had unlocked Ami's fear and anger. The Spirit of God swept through that garden and offered Ami a buoyant liberation. In offering forgiveness, Ami was somehow becoming free.

FEAR OR FORGIVENESS?

There is freedom and peace when we allow God's perfect love to drive out the fear that has kept us in bondage. But for love to have the run of the house, we have to trust that it's more powerful than fear. That's easier said than done. How do we begin to love and forgive those who have deeply wronged us, especially when they don't even recognize the consequences of their actions? I've asked this question myself, and I've had it posed to me countless times in many different forms: "How do I begin to love my alcoholic father who has spent most of his life keeping a bar stool warm and belittling the choices I've made to do God's work?" Or "How do I forgive my pastor for manipulating me and using abusive language to overpower me with his 'spiritual authority'?" Or "How do I love my friend who consistently tears me down through sarcasm and jokes, then ends his self-serving stand-up routine with 'You know I was only kidding'?" When we've been wounded, it's easier to choose self-protection instead of love. But self-protection is a disguise for fear. Our efforts to protect ourselves prevent us from trusting that God can handle our anger, our hurt, our sadness, and our fear.

The only way I've ever been able to move from stubbornness to sensitivity, from arrogance to approachability, from argumentative to agreeable, and from holding a grudge to offering grace is through the act of loving forgiveness. But this does not seem to be an assignment we youth workers are getting gold stars on. Many of us only feel confident when we are in control, and to posture ourselves in a position of forgiveness feels like we've given away what little power we have. There are too many of us who believe the lies that to be humble is to be weak, to seek forgiveness is to lose, to speak the truth in love is too hard and won't be heard. Until we learn to seek forgiveness, offer grace, speak the truth, admit our own wrongs, and bless our enemies, we won't ever be free.

It's irrational to bless someone who has hurt you, yet it sets you free. It's hard to forgive someone who has wounded you deeply, yet it sets you free. It's painful to face your own depravity and ways you have wronged others, yet it sets you free. As 1 John 4:18 reminds us, there is no fear in perfect love—and perfect love is what sets us free.

Soul School Homework

Assignment
A task to be accomplished

Healing Memories

Experiencing forgiveness can bring healing to our past. Read the quote below and spend some time contemplating any experiences, memories, or moments in your story that need the power of forgiveness. Invite a trusted friend to pray with you so that together you can invite God to help you experience forgiveness.

> Forgiving does not mean forgetting. When we forgive a person, the memory of the wound might stay with us for a long time, even throughout our lives. Sometimes we carry the memory in our bodies as a visible sign. But forgiveness changes the way we remember. It converts the curse into a blessing. When we forgive our parents for their divorce, our children for their lack of attention, our friends for their unfaithfulness in crisis, our doctors for their ill advice, we no longer have to experience ourselves as the victims of events we had no control over. Forgiveness allows us to claim our own power and not let these events destroy us; it enables them to become events that deepen the wisdom of our hearts. Forgiveness indeed heals memories.
>
> **—HENRI NOUWEN**

Lab
A place for practice or observation

Freeing Forgiveness

There are experiences in life when we have been hurt or wronged by another person, and it is not possible or desirable for us to contact that person to work though the offense. It is imperative that we not allow ourselves to stay bound up with anger and bitterness. It can be possible to offer forgiveness to a person without needing to meet face to face. Spend some time working through the process below if there is a person you feel God is asking you to forgive.

1. Talk with God about your true feelings, pain, and hurt. Be real and raw about what you are feeling; do not hide your real emotions. Do not make excuses or minimize the offense. Talk with God out loud or in your journal.

2. Ask God to help you see the situation through his perspective and his eyes. (See Psalm 139:23-24.)

3. Confess your own sin to him (contempt, resentment, bitterness, lack of love for the person, etc.)

4. In the presence of God forgive the person/persons for the specific wrong committed. It helps to say this aloud: "I forgive you, _____, for (name the specific hurt/issue)."

5. Ask God to heal your heart emotionally and ask that his love and grace would also be made real to those who have hurt you.

6. Pray for the person who has wounded you.

7. Ask God if you need to talk with this person directly.

Test

A procedure for critical evaluation; a means of determining the presence, quality, or truth of something; a trial

Be Not Afraid

Are there places in your life where you feel afraid of forgiveness? Spend some time answering the questions below to help you determine how fear affects your desire for forgiveness.

1. Do you feel that offering forgiveness to the person who has hurt you justifies the wrongs that were committed and the pain it has caused?

   YES   NO   SOMETIMES

2. Do you want the person who has wronged you to take the first step toward forgiveness?

   YES   NO   SOMETIMES

3. Do you feel like the wrong that has been committed against you does not deserve forgiveness?

   YES   NO   SOMETIMES

4. Are there situations where you know you've committed a wrong against someone but you are too embarrassed or ashamed to seek forgiveness?

   YES   NO   SOMETIMES

5. Do you avoid offering forgiveness because you are afraid that going to the person you have wronged may create a more difficult situation?

   YES   NO   SOMETIMES

If you answered *yes* or *maybe* to any of the questions above, spend some time journaling through your thoughts and emotions. Ask God to allow his perfect love to cast out the fear that keeps you from the freedom that forgiveness can bring.

CHAPTER EIGHT

The Lost Art of Following

Soul Lesson: To be an effective and influential leader, one must first learn how to be a healthy follower.

FOLLOW THE FOLLOWER

We've all played the classic childhood game of "Follow the Leader." Many of us were willing to be followers only in hopes that we would eventually become the leader. But the game is actually won only when you first learn how to follow.

Every leader—inside or outside the church—has been a follower at some point. Unfortunately, too many leaders have forgotten that the same basic skills that make someone a good follower are also needed to be a good leader. Jesus knew what he was asking when he spoke the two simple words, "Follow me." He knew that truly great leaders get formed through the process of healthy submission and following.

SUBMISSION

I have a friend I've known for many years. He is a contagiously dynamic person. He can somehow see the possibilities in the middle of rubble. He's a strategic thinker who's always full of creative ideas—the kind of guy who changes the environment of any room. He's a risk taker who constantly inspires others to jump on his bandwagon of adventurous faith.

I believe my friend loves God and is serious about his desire to do ministry. But as I've watched him over the years, I've noticed a glaring void in his character. He's never truly submitted himself to any other leader, and I'm not sure he has ever embraced the idea of himself as a follower. He's the kind of guy who always has to be in charge of every situation. When we first met, he was working as a youth pastor and had nothing but negativity and criticism for the senior pastor at his church. He worked himself out of that job (translation: he was fired) and then moved on to another position. As he started at his next church, he felt hopeful that the situation would be better—but after about 18 months he found himself sprucing up his resume again.

After 10 years of moving from church to church, he decided he'd had it with bad supervisors. He packed up his family and moved to the West to start his own church. Things started out strong there. He cast a compelling vision, and others followed eagerly. Some people even sold their homes and gave up jobs to join him. The first few years were dynamic and exciting, but as time went on the tension began to increase. My friend who never learned how to be led had no real idea how to lead others. The once-promising ministry started falling apart. Staff members left, donors backed out, and ultimately he walked away from the ministry. His critique and bull-headed commentary on church politics, leadership, and just about any other topic under the sun continue to keep him isolated. Friends and family have started distancing themselves, leaving him alone and bitter on his soapbox of sarcasm. I believe my friend's inability to submit to authority, even if it was "bad leadership," has kept him stagnant and secluded.

FOOLISH FOLLOWING—FOOLISH LEADING

I've met many other youth workers similar to my friend. God has gifted them with many skills, yet they sometimes seem most skilled in ranting and raving about how terrible their leader is—whether it's a supervisor, senior pastor, lay leader in the church, or another authority figure. So many of us have sat behind closed doors, grumbling about the many flaws of our bosses and writing passionate manifestos of how we will do everything so much better when we finally become the leader. But learning to submit to authority is essential if we would ever be healthy leaders.

Following is hard—sometimes much harder than leading. And it's not just when we have an ineffective or less-than-desirable leader that following becomes difficult. Jesus was the perfect leader, yet the disciples still struggled to be good followers— sometimes questioning or rejecting his decisions and priorities. Following means that we learn to submit, and submitting requires a surrendering of the will. But so many of us fight this process and end up becoming foolish followers. And many of the characteristics that are problematic for us as followers also plague us when we later attempt to lead.

So what are some of the characteristics we find among foolish followers who then develop into foolish leaders? Here are three:

Judgment

Foolish following often starts to develop in a follower who is frustrated with his or her leader. These followers look at the poor performance of their leaders and begin to critique leadership they view as less than desirable. If the critiquing turns into ego-tistical judging, a dangerous disease can creep into a follower's heart. When things aren't going the way we want them to go, our human nature seems conditioned to look for someone to blame. So we convict the leader. We start to assume we know the leader's motives. We question his or her capacity. We wonder if anyone else can see what's going on. Furthermore, we often judge our leaders unfairly based on our own limited understanding of the situation, and we self-righteously assume we'd do a much better job if we were in the leadership position. Jesus talked about the danger of judging another person based on limited information: "Stop judging by mere appearances, but instead judge correctly" (John 7:24).

Gossip

Often, when we judge our leader to be inadequate, we follow up that behavior by looking for other judgers. We begin sending out subtle smoke signals to see if anyone else is unhappy with the leadership. We make nonchalant comments to determine if there are other frustrated followers in our midst. If we find other resentful companions, we pool our complaints together and begin to participate in the age-old practice of gossip. Of course, we never call it gossip. We may even hide it under a cloak of spiritual language. We gather under the guise of prayer for our ministry or our leader and end up spending more time talking about the leader's flaws instead of talking to God about how we can help the leader. Or we talk about wanting to "process" or "seek counsel" when our real intent is to swap notes with other dissatisfied followers. Gossip doesn't just build walls between you and your leader; it also reveals to others that you are not a confidence keeper. "A gossip betrays a confidence; so avoid anyone who talks too much" (Proverbs 20:19).

Leaked Frustrations

In addition to judgment and gossip, there are a lot of other subtle ways that foolish followers tend to "leak" their frustrations about their leaders. Some styles of these are easy to detect, like a shift in attitude. Followers can show outward signs of their internal frustration by staying extra quiet and passive. Or they can become overtly strong and aggressive in their demeanor and verbal responses to their leaders. Either of these approaches—one passive, the other aggressive—can create an emotionally charged relationship between the follower and the leader. A follower might also make a private internal decision that they will no longer follow the leader's direction, turning off any healthy sense of submission (even in a difficult situation). While this kind of undermining of one's leader may be harder to detect, it can be just as damaging. It is very difficult to mask bitterness, envy, hurt, and other feelings of frustration that may be lurking in the heart of a frustrated follower. When these are not dealt with in a healthy and direct way, these emotions leak out in more destructive ways. "As water reflects the face, so one's life reflects the heart" (Proverbs 27:19).

WISE FOLLOWING—WISE LEADING

Foolish following is a trap that's easy to fall into. The journey to being a wise follower requires discipline, faithfulness, and time. But those who travel this road of wise following develop characteristics that serve them equally well as leaders.

Honest Communication

One of the most common breakdowns between leaders and followers surrounds communication. Eric was a guy on my staff awhile back who modeled healthy communication. He kept me informed as his leader. He knew the right moments to knock on my office door. He knew what was important to relay in person and what could be communicated effectively through voice mail or e-mail. When he questioned a decision I'd made, he voiced his concern respectfully at an appropriate time. He was honest about what was going on in his life. And when he felt like we weren't hearing each other, he sought clarity. Healthy communication takes time and needs to be consistent. When it's hit-or-miss or too much time lapses between connections, leaders and followers can both make incorrect assumptions about what the other is thinking. Healthy dialogue is always honest, clear, and thoughtful. That doesn't mean that you'll never raise your voice, get angry, or have conflicts. But when the follower is committed both to listening and to communicating his or her feelings in a healthy way that the leader can hear, these problems have a much higher chance of being resolved effectively. Healthy communication is vital if followers and leaders work well together. When we are willing to make the effort to ensure effective communication with our leaders, we will carry that same commitment to healthy dialogue into our own positions of leadership.

Healthy Loyalty

A wise follower also displays a healthy loyalty to his or her leader. For some of us, this is not an easy characteristic to develop, especially if we have leadership talents and strong opinions of our own. Loyalty is the ability to be unwavering in commitment to a person or mission in good times or bad. Loyalty may call out demanding sacrifices on the part of the follower. But leaders often direct most effectively when they sense a steady and enduring loyalty among their staff and volunteers. One of the most faithful and loyal followers I know is my friend Eve. I met Eve when I was hired to lead in a ministry for which she was a volunteer. Her loyalty was already anchored in the ministry. She had many reasons to have her doubts about me as her new leader—she'd had a long line of disappointing leaders in her past. But right away she opened herself up to being led, and in time a deep level of mutual loyalty developed between us. Eve moved from volunteer to intern to staff member to eventually succeeding me in my position in the ministry. Eve's loyalty, as both a follower and a leader, is one of her most inspiring qualities—and it generates a corresponding loyalty among those with whom she works. Eve's style is more simple and subdued than your typical "over the top" youth minister. But her deep commitment to displaying healthy and wise loyalty makes her one of the best followers and leaders I've known.

Keep in mind that loyalty must always be coupled with wisdom. If a leader is asking you to do something that violates your integrity or values, you should always remain true to your internal moral compass and to God as your ultimate authority. But if we develop a true sense of loyalty in our following, our own leadership will cultivate committed followers.

Heartfelt Prayer

One of the most important commitments any of us can make as followers is to pray for those who lead us. Regardless of whether you're thrilled with your present leader or hoping for a new one, your prayer for that person's life and ministry will make a difference in both of your hearts. When we position ourselves in a place of prayer for another person, God has a brilliant and miraculous way of shifting our hearts. I've had many moments as a frustrated follower when praying for the leader over me felt like the last thing I wanted to do. In these times I'd often begin my prayer with a closed and accusing spirit brewing with frustrations, complaints, and suggestions to God about how he should deal with my leader's irresponsibility or immaturity. But once my heart became quiet and open, God would somehow grant me a new perspective on my leader's life. Or God would fill me with compassion for the situation my leader was in. Or God would give me wisdom as to how I could work through my righteous anger and forgive my leader. Prayer can also help us keep an accurate perspective about who our real Leader is. I confess that there have been far too many times when I've given too much weight to an authority figure's opinions and suggestions for my life, forgetting that God is my ultimate authority. When I am in a regular practice of prayer, my perspective on the real role my leader should play stays healthy and appropriately accurate. Prayer is essential to the life of a wise follower, and it must be a staple within any leadership culture you create.

DAVID: WISE FOLLOWER, WISE LEADER

No leader is perfect. It's okay to think your leader has some flaws. Look at the story of David and Saul. The Bible tells us Saul was God's anointed leader. He came from a royal bloodline that had an all-star lineup of Abraham and Moses in it. He was a distinguished and decorated officer who developed battle strategies that defeated the enemy time and time again. He was prophetic and empowered by the Spirit of God, and ultimately was used by God to deliver Israel.

That's quite a list of leadership credentials! Yet in spite of all this, Saul is most remembered as a crazy king. He became arrogant and prideful, and this affected his ability to lead. God's anointing was lifted from him. Saul was plagued with jealousy and rage toward David, who was greatly loved by the people of Israel. Saul literally threw spears at David and tried to hunt him down and take his life. David was under the authority of an imperfect leader, but it was in following this flawed king that the young shepherd, David, became known as a man after God's own heart. David submitted to Saul's absurd authority for years. He found himself spending sleepless nights hiding in dark caves, and surely had moments when he begged God to end his subjection under the reign of such a dysfunctional king. But David nonetheless submitted to the sovereign leader God had placed in charge of Israel, and the character and humility that was woven into David's life during those many difficult years would later play a pivotal role when he was called to lead the same nation.

I believe David is known as a wise leader because he was first a wise follower. God placed David under an imperfect, less-than-desirable, "crazy" king who literally threw spears at him. David could have easily picked up a spear and threw it back. David was so beloved that he probably could have turned the whole army of Israel on Saul. He had the favor of the people but he never used that popularity to hurt Saul. David never became a foolish follower. Even in the darkness of a cave, David never complained, he never judged, he never gossiped. He followed.

The Bible talks more about following than about leading. God calls us all to be followers. And yet so many of us fight against it. We are stubborn. Prideful. Arrogant. Determined. And we often throw spears back.

LIFE-ALTERING FOLLOWING

As April and I sat in the little bagel shop down the street from my home, we held our mugs of coffee close to our faces, hoping the warmth would bring a little relief from the miserable Chicago winter. I'd almost achieved my weird desire to be a "regular" at this little restaurant. The staff there knew that I came there every week and always ordered the same thing: cinnamon sugar bagel (toasted with butter) and a large coffee.

April was one of the first interns I'd ever led. She was 18 years old and had dreams coming out of her toes. She was fresh out of high school—feisty, strong, and confident. She'd just moved to Chicago to become part of our church's new internship program, and she didn't know a soul. Her new home was my guest room and I was her leader. I was new to leading and she was new to following—so we embarked upon the adventure together.

Our conversations over bagels were among my favorite moments of the week. She was passionate, filled with ideas, great with students, and she loved Jesus. The only problem was that April was incredibly stubborn and reluctant to follow. She had a tenacious untamed spirit that could stand some healthy bridling. So over our bagels and coffee one morning, I decided to talk with April about this. It was incredibly difficult to tell my wide-eyed young friend who was just starting out in ministry that she'd never be a good leader if she didn't learn to become a healthy follower. But I told her how her pride and ego were preventing her from having the teachable spirit she needed in order to grow. Her silence was like a slow dripping faucet as she took in my critiques—and then I watched her eyes begin to swell with puddles of tears.

That day, we had a life-altering conversation laced with confession, grace, accountability, and hope. And in the years that followed, I watched April became one of the most faithful followers I've ever had the privilege of leading. She regularly engaged in honest communication with me. She showed healthy loyalty, and I'm confident she was committed to praying for me regularly. In fact, when I was invited later to lead a new student ministry at our church, April was the first person I hired.

I was capable of having that conversation with April only because I'd once been part of a similar conversation with one of my leaders. In my early days of student ministry I was much like April—passionate, determined, driven, ambitious, and full of hopes and dreams for ministry. But like April when I first met her, my drive to lead was not matched by an equally strong commitment to be a healthy follower. Thankfully, I had a leader willing to sit across from me and lovingly challenge me to learn to submit in healthy and honorable ways.

I'm not sure what your situation is. Maybe there's a place in your life where you find it hard to follow. Perhaps you're struggling in an area where you know you need to submit, but you've not done so. Maybe you're not even sure why the leader you serve is even in a position of authority at all. I've certainly had moments when I struggled to figure out why God would ever choose the person I was following to become a leader. But I find great hope in the fact that God doesn't ask my opinion on his decisions. He simply invites me to trust that he is always in control. And I've found that, even when I've been under a leader I wouldn't have chosen, God has used that experience to reflect back to me parts of my own character that need to grow and be challenged.

Learning to follow and submit has been one of the most productive greenhouses for my own growth and development. So maybe those of us who desire to reach our full potential need to recall the game we played many years ago, and learn again how to follow the leader.

Soul School Homework

Assignment
A task to be accomplished

Dear...

Spend some time thinking about a leader who's had a positive impact on your life. What were some of this leader's characteristics that left a positive impression? If this person is still accessible to you, spend some time writing him or her a letter of encouragement and then send it.

Soul School Homework

Assignment
A task to be accomplished

Dear...

Spend some time thinking about a leader who's had a positive impact on your life. What were some of this leader's characteristics that left a positive impression? If this person is still accessible to you, spend some time writing him or her a letter of encouragement and then send it.

Lab
A place for practice or observation

Take Up Your Cross

"Anyone who won't shoulder his own cross and follow behind me can't be my disciple."

—LUKE 14:27

Consider these precise, strong, and convicting words from Jesus about following. Spend some time in prayer and meditation asking God to reveal to you the kind of follower you are, and ask him to transform you into the kind of follower he longs for you to be.

Test

A procedure for critical evaluation; a means of determining the presence, quality, or truth of something; a trial

What Kind of Follower Are You?

Answer the questions below to evaluate your behavior as a follower.

1. Do you pray regularly for your leader?

Often				Sometimes				Never	
10	9	8	7	6	5	4	3	2	1

2. Are you open to accepting direction and critique from your leader?

Often				Sometimes				Never	
10	9	8	7	6	5	4	3	2	1

3. Are you willing to give your leader and others in authority credit and public recognition?

Often				Sometimes				Never	
10	9	8	7	6	5	4	3	2	1

4. When your leader makes a decision you disagree with, do you go to the leader with your frustration and engage in healthy communication?

Often				Sometimes				Never	
10	9	8	7	6	5	4	3	2	1

5. Can you provide constructive feedback to your leader without undermining his or her authority?

Often   **Sometimes**   **Never**

10   9   8   7   6   5   4   3   2   1

_____ Add the numbers above. Look below to see your grade.

50 – 35

A - You are a healthy follower—and these same skills serve you well as a leader. Keep it up!

34 – 20

C - You are an adequate follower. Continue looking for ways you can grow and improve!

Less than 20

F - You are a failing follower. Pray in an ongoing way that God would help you overcome your inability to follow, or it will be a major obstacle in your life and ministry!

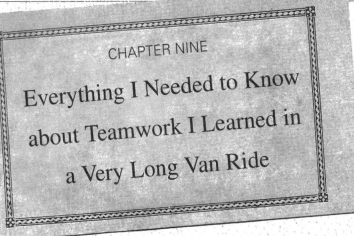

CHAPTER NINE

Everything I Needed to Know about Teamwork I Learned in a Very Long Van Ride

Soul Lesson: Our selfish egos are the opponent of healthy communal ministry.

FROM KICKBALL TO MINISTRY

Standing in the schoolyard at recess and hoping I'd be picked for an impromptu game of kickball is probably my earliest memory of desperately desiring to be on a team. As the captains picked players one by one, I so wanted to be chosen—and I hoped even more that I would land on the winning team. Very little has changed since then. When it comes to ministry, I still love being on a team, and it's even better when I feel I'm on a winning team.

I was just 22 years old when I wandered into my first real ministry team at my local church. I had little experience and didn't know a thing about student ministry (*though* I thought I did). But I loved God, loved students, and asked if the church needed any volunteers in its high school ministry. Like most churches, they were desperate for volunteers ("If you have a pulse, then you're qualified to serve.") So after a few interviews, I started volunteering in the student ministry. I loved it. I felt alive and excited about the relationships I was building with students and other leaders.

After I'd volunteered for a little while, the director of the ministry asked me if I'd consider joining the full-time staff. I was honored, to say the least, and thrilled to be able to take on a larger role in such a great team. At that time they'd just lost the woman who kept everything organized. They didn't *misplace* her—she actually had a little breakdown and left because she couldn't handle the pressure of the job. They needed someone to take her role—so that became my job. I was the administrator. I tend to be a fairly organized person, but I don't enjoy being in charge of all the details. But that was the job they needed me to do, so I gave it my best shot. It was up to me to make sure things ran smoothly—and that included everything from managing the budget to ordering the pizza to taking kids to the ER when they cracked their heads open playing full-contact Frisbee golf. If you imagine spending an entire day only using your non dominant hand to accomplish your tasks, then you get a sense of how I felt most days while doing my job. I had a deep desire to do my job well, but I was regularly frustrated and felt I was constantly letting down the rest of the team.

I remember one day when I was in my office counting the money we'd made at a recent fundraiser. One of the guys on my team came in, wanting to chat and catch up. I was feeling stressed out and insecure about the job I was doing. He noticed my tension and said, "Hey, are you okay? You seem a little overwhelmed."

He was probably sorry he asked, because his question opened up the gates: "*A little* overwhelmed? Let's try *a lot*. I don't know what I'm doing. I'm tired and stressed out, no one is helping me, I feel like I have to do everything by myself, and I don't know why I can't stop crying." The guy looked scared out of his mind. Having no idea what to do with my explosive emotions, he kindly patted me on the shoulder, left my office, and shut the door. The rest of the day no one came to my office—and I later learned this was because he'd jokingly put a note on my door that read, "Jeanne is really PMSing. Do not disturb." We all had a good laugh about it at the end of the day. But what was really going on inside me was that my ego was overwhelmed by a deep fear of failure. Eventually my leader changed my position to get me in a spot that better suited my talents. But I needed to do some serious Soul School work with all that was living just beneath the surface. My ego was so consumed with pride that I didn't want to admit I needed help in my job. And that was the primary reason I was feeling hindered and handicapped. The team wasn't getting the best of who I was and what I had to offer. My pride was keeping me closed off, preventing me from letting my teammates into some of the struggles I was facing. I needed to let them into my life and acknowledge how my ego was hindering our team.

LACE UP THE GLOVES

That first ministry team I served on was by and large a healthy one—trust was high, people could disagree and debate yet still feel safe, and our lives were shared with openness and vulnerability. But over the years I've also been on unhealthy teams where there's a dangerous level of competition, gossip happens, time gets wasted, people jump to conclusions about one another, and trust is nowhere to be found. Being on both kinds of teams has led to my commitment that I will never do ministry outside the context of community. But to live in healthy community with one another requires the discipline of safely shining the light on our tender egos that prefer to stay in the dark.

I know every story is unique—and the challenges you're facing with regard to doing ministry in a team setting may differ from the challenges I've faced. But over the years I've observed that the primary attribute that separates healthy teams from unhealthy ones is the ego of the team members. The ego issues that we tend to think of as personal and internal actually affect the health of any team. For teams to be healthy and highly functioning, each of its members needs to lace up the boxing gloves and get into the ring against his or her own self-consumed ego—which is the opponent to trust, honesty, and purpose on a team.

Round 1: Ego vs. Trust

One of my favorite writers about teamwork is Patrick Lencoini. In his fabulous book *The Five Dysfunctions of a Team*, he says, "Trust lies at the heart of a functioning, cohesive team. Without it, teamwork is all but impossible." I couldn't agree more. So many of us tend to think of trust as something we need to earn from others and others need to gain from us. We make trust an external commodity that can be given and gained, with us as the primary dealer. But this short-sided view of trust misses the deeper essence of how trust is produced from within. Real trust on a team begins with its members committing themselves to living in ways that are vulnerable, honest, and self-aware. Because of our egos, many of us are afraid to let others see our flaws and flubs—so we spend the majority of our time and energy covering and protecting a false facade that we think others would never want to trust. Because of our egos, when we're asked, "How are you? Do you need any help? Is everything okay?" we give the dangerous response of "Fine"—even when we are feeling desperate inside. Because of our egos, we judge and doubt the intentions of others and make assumptions about what our teammates can and can't do. Because of our egos, many teams end up dallying and delaying tasks, as team members all center their activity on managing the assumed behaviors of others. When it comes to knocking out trust on a team, each team member's broken ego is a heavyweight contender.

Awhile back our student ministry team took some core students on a camping trip. More than a few things went wrong; in fact, it was clear pretty early on that this trip was going to be a complete debacle. As the team leader I was frustrated—and I've never had a good poker face when it comes to hiding my emotions. It was obvious that I was disappointed with how things were going. On the first night of the weekend, one of my team members and I were discussing how we could salvage the event and make the best of the rest of the weekend. As we sat talking around the campfire, he uttered a phrase in passing that stopped me in my leadership tracks: "You know, Jeanne, the rest of the team is so afraid of letting you down." I was shocked. But as I sought to understand why he'd say this, he lovingly offered many examples of a reality I'd never allowed myself to acknowledge. I'd played a major role in creating a fear of failure on our team. Because of my ego-ridden drive to be perfect, and my unhealthy desire never to let others down, I'd created a team environment where other members of the team didn't really feel safe and able to trust me—or one another.

This realization utterly broke me. I was wrecked over the fact that I'd been living with and then leading our team toward a lack of trust. I took some time to contemplate the truth of what I was now seeing for the first time. I grieved over my actions and began to ask God for a picture of how to lead from a place of trust instead of my selfish ego. I gathered my team and sought their forgiveness and then started throwing the right punches to knock out my own selfish ego. As the leader I needed to value trust on our team above my own ego-driven desires. I needed to do some personal soul work. I made a commitment to engage in regular conversations and practices of trust—some of which included getting uncomfortable. But I realized that by not being vulnerable with our team, I'd created an environment where the other team members didn't feel they could be vulnerable with one another. So everyone was protecting his or her own ego.

I didn't change overnight. Our team wasn't suddenly a well-bonded trusting team. But over time trust began to surface, and egos began to fade.

Round 2: Ego vs. Honesty

I think one of the worst things that could ever be said about a team is that its members always agree and get along. I don't know why we think that niceness and harmony are such elevated spiritual gifts—but there are far too many Christians doing ineffective ministry because of this myth. Some of my favorite moments from the recorded life of Jesus come when he's smack dab in the middle of a conflict. You never see him trying to just make everyone happy and cover up the tension. Instead, he usually launches right into the issue—typically adding even more tension. I love the story of when Jesus and the disciples are on their way to Jerusalem, and he once again reminds them that he is going to be put to death and then be resurrected three days later (Mark 10:32-41). Instead of feeling compassion and sadness over what Jesus is about to face, James and his brother, John, see this as an opportunity to ask Jesus for a special seat of honor in heaven. The rest of the disciples overhear this request and they get all bent out of shape. Jesus could have just let the issue blow over, but instead he confronts what is really going on among his disciples by saying:

> "You know that those who are regarded as rulers of the Gentiles lord it
> over them, and their high officials exercise authority over them. Not so
> with you. Instead, whoever wants to become great among you must be
> your servant, and whoever wants to be first must be slave of all. For even
> the Son of Man did not come to be served, but to serve, and to give his
> life as a ransom for many."
>
> **—MARK 10:42–45**

Jesus did not avoid the conflict; in fact, he walked right into it. Yet so many of us when faced with a conflict on our team turn and walk the other way as if we didn't even notice it. It could be that our egos will feel bruised if we're forced to admit that our teams don't always function as well as we'd like. Or maybe we're not ready to acknowledge our own role in the conflict. It could be an internal fear of not wanting to engage in a difficult conversation. Maybe we just want to "keep the peace." Or perhaps we've never had healthy conflict modeled to us. But anytime we allow our own broken inner egos to dictate how we deal with conflict, we lose the opportunity for growth that comes from engaging in honest conversation.

Pop Quiz

When was the last time you faced a situation of conflict? Did you confront it directly and honestly? Why or why not?

I know of a guy who has been the student ministry leader at a particular church for almost a decade. He landed his role when the church was small and just starting out, and he's barely held the ministry together. There haven't been any major catastrophes—but the ministry has remained stagnant and there's constant turnover on the leadership team because volunteers and staff keep leaving. It is quite evident to many other leaders in the church that he's not in the best position, but they are reluctant to remove him because he's been there since the church began. Their own fear of having an honest dialogue has kept an entire ministry suffering.

I know of a young woman who directs the marketing department of a nonprofit ministry. She's incredibly talented and deeply committed to what she does. Her supervisor is a hard-driving, results-oriented, boundary-less leader who constantly asks her to do more. Because of some brokenness in her own ego and her fear of saying no, she continues to jump through every hoop he puts in front of her. She's grown tired and frustrated with her supervisor, but her fearful ego keeps her from engaging in a healthy and honest conversation about the conflict in their working relationship.

So many leaders are afraid of honest conflict. Our egos have become so padded and protected from avoiding healthy contention that, when we are forced to have to deal with a problem or disagreement, we often fumble. Erik was a guy on my staff team who grew up in a family that avoided conflict at all costs. When he joined our staff team, Erik and I had a couple of intense conversations that felt clarifying and defining to me, but they felt agonizing for him. I noticed his tension and asked him why he felt so uncomfortable with our conversation. As he relayed the story of his family and how they dealt with conflict (or, more accurately, avoided it), I began to see how difficult it was for him to move past how he had been trained to believe all conflict was bad. Over many years of working together, I watched him make tremendous strides toward overcoming his fear of honest conflict. In a letter of encouragement that he wrote to me many years later, he shared that our working relationship had helped him learn how to be in conflict with someone *because* you care about that person. Our teams will only become effective if team members commit to engaging in honest conversations with one another—even when we passionately disagree.

Round 3: Ego vs. Purpose

Growing up in Chicago I was surrounded by some of the most loyal sports fans in America. There is no such thing as a fair-weather fan in Chicago (maybe because there's not a whole lot of fair weather!) The commitment, unyielding support, and love Chicago fans have for their sports teams is almost patriotic. Being in Chicago during the early '90s when the Bulls won the NBA title three straight years was like living in Camelot. The city was united in pride. Of course, that team was known for its most spectacular player, Michael Jordan—but he did not win those championships alone. He was part of a talented team that was devoted to the common purpose of winning. I love what Phil Jackson, the Bulls' former coach, once said, "The strength of the team is each individual member...the strength of each member is the team." When a team knows each member's unique contribution, and when the members together commit to a combined purpose, individual egos usually won't get in the way. But when team members are focused on their own agendas and seek to use the team for their own gain, both the individuals and the team end up losing.

Lack of purpose on any team is frustrating, but it's almost as destructive when a team's direction is being defined by the ego-driven ambitions of a leader or another team member. Great teams are made up of healthy individuals who let go of their own self-inspired agendas for the greater hope of the team's collective vision. This is beautifully demonstrated in the life of Jesus, who entered the planet in the ultimate posture of humility, as a baby. He was equal in status to God, but he didn't seek to use that to benefit himself. Instead, he became a servant and invited others into the purpose of his Father. He didn't make his life all about himself; instead he poured dreams into the hearts of a bunch of young followers who would one day unite to form the church. Jesus modeled how to release one's own ego and put others first.

Do nothing out of selfish ambition or vain conceit. Rather, in humility value others above yourselves, not looking to your own interests but each of you to the interests of the others.

—PHILIPPIANS 2:3-4

When you consider your role in ministry, is your primary purpose to be a servant, or do you have other ego-driven desires and plans that precede this intention? Do you view other members of your team as partners or do you see them as people positioned to carry out your direction? Do you find yourself regularly contemplating how you can advance your own dreams for ministry or are you more energized by garnering the gifts and abilities of your teammates toward a selfless purpose? Self-consumed egos obsessed with advancement always get in the way of a healthy team.

CHURCH VANS CAN CHANGE THE WORLD

A close friend of mine runs a camp in Colorado that takes groups on team-building expeditions. The camping experience includes a wide range of activities—from high ropes to white-water rafting to different service opportunities—all designed to help participants develop a stronger sense of team. As we were catching up a few years ago and he was telling me about his camp, I started wondering if this kind of camping experience might shine a more intentional light on some of the dynamics of our student ministry team. Our calendars were all full, the summer was coming to an end, we had very little money or time, and we were getting ready to rev up another ministry season—but somehow we managed to get all the details in place for a trip. As we were making final preparations to go, each staff member received a sheet of paper with some basic instructions about the weekend—but the primary directive was printed at the bottom of the page: "Please make sure you are in a healthy place

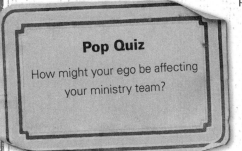

Pop Quiz

How might your ego be affecting your ministry team?

physically, emotionally, spiritually, and relationally. We need you to be you. Nothing more...Nothing less."

We met at the church on a Friday morning at 6:00 a.m. With Starbucks in hand and droopy eyes, the members of our staff team piled into our not-so-pimped-out white church van. We drove all day and most of the night to reach our destination. The guidelines of the experience said that we were not allowed to talk about our ministry. We didn't strategize about what was ahead. We didn't look over our calendar to see if we had all the events in place. We didn't talk about what we wanted to change about the ministry. The whole weekend was designed to help our team members learn how to better trust, communicate, and honor one another's particular contributions.

Every team develops its own unique collective personality. This particular team had great chemistry. Our ability to laugh and have fun came easily. We had the normal quirks and faced different bumps and bruises as any team would, but we always managed to enjoy the experience of working together. We entered the weekend with fairly healthy relationships with one another. But after we spent four straight days moving from van to ropes courses to rapids to van again, something had changed about our team.

When we retell the stories from that weekend, they are almost always exaggerated to the nth degree. Like a silver-haired grandfather spinning tales of the "good old days," our team recounts those two 12-hour van rides and the 22 hours on the ground as one of our greatest experiences together. We got to see one another as we really were. We laughed hard and many shed tears. We created memories. We talked about areas where we struggle with trust. We spoke about past conflicts that had never been fully resolved. We shared our dreams and stories with one another. As we inhaled and exhaled the same oxygen in our cramped 12-passenger van, we somehow became real to one another. The idea of being a healthy functioning team became more energizing than being a collection of individuals each trying to accomplish his or her own purpose. Our own self-consuming egos, fears, and insecurities faded as we honestly shared our lives with one another.

When we returned home from the trip, we still had the normal tensions of ministry and the common miscommunications that arise on any team. But there was a renewed commitment in each of us to put our individual egos aside for the sake of our team. Our communication was flavored with greater grace and honesty. We trusted one another more fully and supported each other's individual roles. We were united around a single purpose and hope for the ministry. We believed in what we were doing together. Somehow, what happened in that van made us really believe that by working together we could begin to change our little corner of the world.

It's a simple truth you've known since grade school: You'll never win at kickball if you try to play by yourself, no matter how good you might think you are. You need a team. And the same is true about ministry—it's always better as part of a team.

Soul School Homework

Assignment
A task to be accomplished

Duke It Out

Spend some time thinking about the last conflict that you experienced on your team. Write out how the conflict might have been resolved differently if every member of the team were deeply committed to the values of trust, honesty, and purpose.

Lab
A place for practice, observation, or testing

Meditation

Spend some time reading and meditating on this passage of Scripture. What might God be trying to say to you about your own ego?

> My counsel is this: Live freely, animated and motivated by God's Spirit. Then you won't feed the compulsions of selfishness. For there is a root of sinful self-interest in us that is at odds with a free spirit, just as the free spirit is incompatible with selfishness. These two ways of life are antithetical, so that you cannot live at times one way and at times another way according to how you feel on any given day. Why don't you choose to be led by the Spirit and so escape the erratic compulsions of a law-dominated existence?
>
> It is obvious what kind of life develops out of trying to get your own way all the time: repetitive, loveless, cheap sex; a stinking accumulation of mental and emotional garbage; frenzied and joyless grabs for happiness; trinket gods; magic-show religion; paranoid loneliness; cutthroat competition; all-consuming-yet-never-satisfied wants; a brutal temper; an impotence to love or be loved; divided homes and divided lives; small-minded and lopsided pursuits; the vicious habit of depersonalizing everyone into a rival; uncontrolled and uncontrollable addictions; ugly parodies of community. I could go on.
>
> This isn't the first time I have warned you, you know. If you use your freedom this way, you will not inherit God's kingdom.

But what happens when we live God's way? He brings gifts into our lives, much the same way that fruit appears in an orchard—things like affection for others, exuberance about life, serenity. We develop a willingness to stick with things, a sense of compassion in the heart, and a conviction that a basic holiness permeates things and people. We find ourselves involved in loyal commitments, not needing to force our way in life, able to marshal and direct our energies wisely.

—GALATIANS 5:16-23 (*The Message*)

What is this passage saying to you about life in community?

Test

A procedure for critical evaluation; a means of determining the presence, quality, or truth of something; a trial

Le-go My Ego

Answer the questions below to see how much your ego may be damaging your team.

1. When a job is too big or overwhelming for you, are you willing to ask for help?

Often				**Sometimes**				**Never**	
10	9	8	7	6	5	4	3	2	1

2. Do you allow yourself to be vulnerable enough to share personal issues in your life with your coworkers?

Often				**Sometimes**				**Never**	
10	9	8	7	6	5	4	3	2	1

3. When you have a conflict with another member of the team, do you seek to resolve it quickly and directly rather than just dwelling on it internally?

Often				**Sometimes**				**Never**	
10	9	8	7	6	5	4	3	2	1

4. Do you feel a sense of unhealthy competition with other members of the team?

Often				**Sometimes**				**Never**	
10	9	8	7	6	5	4	3	2	1

5. Do you feel like your purpose on the team is more important than other's purposes?

Often				**Sometimes**				**Never**	
10	9	8	7	6	5	4	3	2	1

6. Do you regularly pray for the goals your team is trying to accomplish?

Often				**Sometimes**				**Never**	
10	9	8	7	6	5	4	3	2	1

CHAPTER TEN

Equal Opportunity Authorship

Soul Lesson: Coauthorship is the only way real ministry will happen. Just as God invites each of us to join him in writing the life he's given us all, we need to learn to share the pen with others as we cowrite our stories of life and ministry.

THE SAINT IN 14C

Anyone who travels frequently has learned some of the unwritten but essential rules to traveling. If you have a connecting flight, the odds of your luggage arriving at your final destination are slim to none—so take everything on board with you. If you are not part of the "superior group" of people deemed "First Class," then try to get a seat in an exit row—you'll have a few more inches of legroom and the added benefit of being the first one out the emergency door if there's a crisis. Another helpful unwritten rule: When an airline employee asks you, "Has your luggage been with you at all times?"—that's not the time to work on your stand-up comedy routine and playfully mention, "Yes, except for when that mysterious guy dropped a package in it. Ha, ha, ha." You'll likely spend the rest of your day—maybe the rest of your week—being questioned by authorities who don't think you have a future in comedy.

There's one other unwritten rule many frequent flyers quietly adhere to: If you see a parent traveling with small children, sit as far away from them as you possibly can. Otherwise, the odds of you sitting next to a child who wants to use every little device in your row of seats as a new toy are very high. I have to admit that I used to be one of these travelers. I had all kinds of sneaky and subtle ways of finding out which rows the parents and children were sitting in and then changing my seat so I was as far away as possible. I used to stare in amazement at the tattered moms and dads lugging their baby paraphernalia through the airport like tired soldiers who'd been marching with heavy packs all night. My respect was through the roof for these honorable parents willing to take on the challenge of traveling with small children. I just didn't want to be sitting near them on the plane.

My son took his first plane ride at five weeks old, and if he qualified for frequent flyer miles, he might have racked up a free trip within his first year. It was hard for me to become the kind of traveler I'd always avoided. Don't get me wrong, I absolutely love being a mother—but I absolutely hate traveling on a plane with a small child, especially when I'm alone. When I'm forced to do this, I have a whole new set of travel tactics. Now I scope out the terminal for the most sensitive, patient, grandmotherly-looking person on my flight, and try to get my seat near hers.

> Reading and writing our story becomes a lonely affair if it's done outside of community. Stories are meant to be told, heard, and retold with others.
>
> —DAN ALLENDER

A little while back I was traveling with my 15-month-old son, Elijah. He was fascinated with everything that was happening on the plane. He sat on my lap and watched as the other passengers moved past our row. He said hello to everyone who got on the plane. With his cute wave and high-pitched voice, he was quite adorable. I felt like we were starting out the flight making friends. I was feeling good about the flight ahead—until the pilot came over the intercom and informed us that the plane had some mechanical complications that needed to be repaired, and we'd need to wait for a while before we could take off. Our initial good relationship with the other passengers turned sour quickly as Elijah grew impatient. Before long, I'd exhausted every single mommy magic trick I could think of to entertain him. We'd played with the window shade, the armrest, the tray-table, the light switch, and the air vent. I'd gone through my two Ziplocs of Cheerios and goldfish. The sippy cup had somehow fallen and rolled under a few rows in front of us. The toys I'd strategically packed thinking they would occupy him for hours were exhausted in mere minutes. The magazine in the pouch in front of us didn't have nearly enough pictures to keep my son's interest. Elijah was wired with energy. He wanted to run and play and talk...loudly. I felt alone, exhausted, and in need of some relief.

That's when a kind woman next to me sensed my stress and said, "I have three granddaughters. Don't worry—this is nothing." She began to play with Elijah, holding him for a few moments after he literally climbed over me to get to her. She sang him songs, told him stories, and stepped in to help right when I was feeling about ready to break. When we finally reached our destination, she asked a gentleman seated across from us to carry my bags so I could get Elijah in his stroller. She stepped up to the plate right when I was getting ready to strike out with patience. She reassured me that what I was doing was hard and helped me not feel alone. For a few hours she helped me better love what is most precious to me in this world—my little boy.

Initially, I'm sure my determined and dysfunctional being gave off a vibe that said everything was okay—"I don't need any help... I'm perfectly capable of handling my own energetic child while flying across the country." But that's not at all what I was feeling inside. I felt insecure, wondering if I looked incapable of handling my child. I felt alone trying to manage all of his needs. I felt like we were bothering the other passengers, ruining the flying experience for everyone around us. I needed assistance, but I was afraid to ask for it. I didn't want to admit my need for help. When the saint seated in 14C started to help even without my invitation, I felt rescued—and in a strange way, I felt like I had a partner. My son's experience on the plane got better, my experience on the plane get better, and the plane experience of everyone around us got better.

But why was I so reluctant to ask for help? My mom often tells me one of the first phrases I learned to say as a small child was "I can do it." I was insistent on doing things myself. My independent streak developed early on. And while basic independence is incredibly healthy, too much of it causes us to forget we were created to travel through life with others. My desire to do things on my own has affected every area of my life. From family, to friendships, to my marriage, to ministry—my determination and overachieving, self-oriented ways, while they can be strengths and gifts, have also been used in unproductive and hurtful ways.

INDEPENDENT OR INCLUSIVE?

It's mind-blowing to me that the God of the universe, the Creator who formed us from dirt and breathed life into us, did so in the context of community. God, who is one with the Son and the Spirit, designed us within the inclusive relationship of the Trinity. The One who began the composition of our lives shared the writing responsibility within a holy relational community. What is even more mysterious is that God invites each of us to pick up the pen and share in cowriting his or her own story. God doesn't ask us to permanently shift into neutral and wait for him to dictate our every move. He leads us and guides our steps, but he also invites us to shape our stories. God is not so independent that he is unwilling to let us share in directing the plot. The beautiful truth is that God invites us into the process of becoming coauthors of our own stories. His openness to sharing with us how the story goes evokes freedom to dream and envision lives that are completely alive.

We serve an equal opportunity author who welcomes us as coauthors. If the God of the universe welcomes our help in writing our stories, why do few of us ever invite others to share in writing the stories of our lives and ministries? So many of us remain independent, self-determined, and afraid to ask for help. God never meant for us to write our stories alone. He didn't design us to live or minister in isolation. Yet so many of us plan ministry events by ourselves. We don't delegate anything important for fear it may not happen the way we want it to. We don't invite volunteers to do meaningful ministry tasks; instead, we give them mindless roles that barely require showing up. We have men and women throughout our churches who would probably love to be part of the student ministry, but we feel more comfortable holding on to our complaints that there is no one out there to help. There is a part of us that resists and avoids the very thing we were intended for.

I feel like I've been having the same conversation over many years with countless different youth workers. We begin discussing our work, and before long I start hearing phrases like, "I feel alone…" "It's just me…" "We don't have enough (or any) volunteers…" Often this is the reality for many youth workers. And I think the deep desire in each of these statements is the hope that we'll be able to share the ministry we feel called to with people we love. Yet many of us are not doing that. Instead, we are writing the story alone.

WHY WE AVOID TOGETHER

Obviously, we want the ministries we invest our lives in to be effective. We're working with kids because we care about them and we want our efforts to make a difference. And most of us know our ministries could be enriched and deepened if more people were involved. So why do we so often try to go it alone?

Exposure

Many of us avoid bringing others into the writing of our lives and ministries because we fear being exposed. We keep the parts of ourselves we don't want others to know about creatively hidden. We feel safe in the self-protected life we've created for ourselves, and there's a part of us that just wants to keep things the way they've always been. We feel a false sense of security because no one else knows about our disorganized "personal" closets. I think we convince ourselves that it's better to keep the less attractive pieces of ourselves in the dark rather than bringing them out in the open. We don't want to expose our junk because we've found a way to function with it (or in spite of it). We avoid letting others in on our secrets because then we'll need to change the way we've been living—and many of us are too independent to want to change.

I've watched youth workers who have no business trying to manage all of the details of a ministry continue to do it themselves because they don't want to be exposed as someone who needs help with details. I've watched youth workers stand in front of students and labor through a message no one is paying attention to because they don't want to admit they're not really wired up to be great communicators—and this may prevent someone else from using his or her gifts in that area. I've watched youth workers try to encourage adult leaders and students toward a life of authenticity and vulnerability, all the while keeping things about themselves hidden in order to avoid anyone getting too close. Whenever we choose an independence that refuses to allow others to know us as we really are, we miss out on God's intent for us to live and minister in community with others.

Mine

After a young child learns to say a few basic words like "Daddy," "Mommy," and "No," the word "Mine" is usually lurking just around the vocabulary corner. Kids develop their selfish streak early on when it comes to sharing their belongings with others. Many of us have never grown out of this attachment to the word "mine." We view ministry through these same selfish lenses. Many times over the years, I've caught myself talking about "MY ministry" or "MY small group" or "MY gifts" or "MY role." We have a way of clinging to the ministry we are part of as if it's a piece of personal property. That tight grip of control keeps us from seeing that God invites us to share in ministry—not be solo owners of it. God is the original writer of our lives and our ministries; we are contributing authors.

I've met so many youth workers who see student ministry as their personal possession. It plays out in how they view and treat other people who are part of that ministry. They see the volunteers as people there to help accomplish their plans, so they never really empower them to really lead or shape the vision of the ministry. They see the parents as people who complicate their plans, so these youth workers don't try to partner or communicate with parents, which builds up walls of miscommunication and frustration. They see students as attendance numbers to report to their supervisors, so they don't try to truly meet the spiritual, emotional, relational, developmental, and physical needs of those youth. When we take control of what should be shared, we move into the dangerous territory of narcissistic behavior. Whenever we choose a spirit of selfish independence over interdependence and inclusivity, we miss out on God's intent for us to live and minister in community with others.

Competition

My love of winning began at a young age. I've never stood at a starting line content to just do my best. I've never unfolded a board game hoping I'd come in second or third place. I've never auditioned for a play hoping I'd be given a supporting role, or tried out for a sports team hoping to sit the bench. I've always had a competitive spirit. Sometimes this competitiveness has motivated me to work hard and commit myself to tasks in front of me. But my desire to own every property on the Monopoly board (with hotels on each one) also has a dark side. My competitive nature has of-

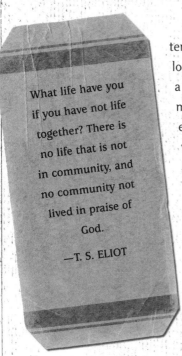

> What life have you if you have not life together? There is no life that is not in community, and no community not lived in praise of God.
>
> —T. S. ELIOT

ten crept into the ministry I do. There have been times when I have looked at other larger ministries and I've masked my jealousy with a determined spirit to work harder and get bigger. There are far too many moments when I have watched other communicators whose every message seems effortlessly packed with great humor and convicting truth—and instead of celebrating their abilities, I've driven myself to try to be better than they are. I've observed other leaders who excel in areas where I struggle, but instead of posturing myself to learn from their strengths, I choose to look for their flaws. My healthy motivation for growth gets junked up with my unhealthy competitive spirit.

I'm not saying that all competitiveness is dysfunctional, because I believe there are some very healthy forms of competition that can help us develop as people and leaders. But competition can be incredibly dangerous in ministry when it becomes a barrier to our relationships with others. When we operate from a spirit of competitiveness, we see the members of our community as opponents instead of partners. Our competitive drive causes us to play power games and engage in "ministry politics" that turn ministry into a win-lose scenario. Whenever we choose a spirit of competitive independence over the freedom that comes from working as an inclusive ministry team, we miss out on God's intent for us to live and minister in community with others.

REAL MINISTRY AND LIFE HAPPEN ONLY IN COMMUNITY

When I began reflecting upon my experience with the saint in 14C, I realized that there is a lie that I've too often followed in life and ministry. It goes something like this: *Showing others that you are capable, strong, and independent is vital to achievement in life and ministry.* It is humbling for me to write those words and ponder the sober reality that many pages in my life and ministry story were written under the motivation of that self-serving lie. The kindness and gentle help of the woman in 14C called forth a deeper desire within me that longs to admit when I feel weak, incapable, and in need of others. When she offered her help and assistance, she reminded me I was doing something very difficult and I needed support. For a few short hours within the very cramped quarters of that airplane, she picked up the pen and we coauthored a few pages of the story together.

We are designed from community for the purpose of community. We have not tasted real life or real ministry if we have been wandering through the landscape of our stories alone. And the ministries we are part of will not guide young people to life unless they are lead by people who are committed to community.

So what is it that keeps you from letting others share in your story? Are you avoiding exposure? Are you afraid to let someone else play in your private ministry sandbox? Are you so determined to win that you didn't even notice that it's not a competition? There are men and women throughout our churches who are waiting to be invited into our stories and the stories of our ministry. There are men and women who would make fabulous mentors or small group leaders or teachers or worship leaders or friends to students who hunger for adults who will show them love and do life alongside them. So are you willing to pass the pen and let them start writing the story with you?

Soul School Homework

Assignment
A task to be accomplished

To Need, or Not To Need: That is the Question

Consider the following questions:

How would you describe a needy person?

How do you feel about needy people?

Describe an area of your life where you have a hard time asking for help. Can you articulate why you don't want the assistance of someone else?

Is there an experience in your life that taught you that independence was better than being dependent on others?

How could admitting your own need help produce spiritual maturity in you?

Lab
A place for practice or observation

Share the Burden

"Carry each other's burdens, and in this way you will fulfill the law of Christ. If any of you think you are something when you are nothing, you deceive yourselves."

—GALATIANS 6:2-3

Spend some time contemplating this passage. Think about a burden you have been carrying alone. Who could help carry it with you? What is this passage saying to you about life in community?

Test

A procedure for critical evaluation; a means of determining the presence, quality, or truth of something; a trial

Yes, No, or Maybe?

EXPOSURE

Is there anything you've kept hidden from others that you know you need to share with your community?

Yes   No   Maybe

MINE

Are there aspects of the ministry you are part of that you are doing yourself because you are either afraid or too selfish to give away to others?

Yes   No   Maybe

COMPETITION

Are there any people with whom you feel an unhealthy competitiveness?

Yes   No   Maybe

If you answered yes or maybe to any of the questions above, think of something you can do this next week to help you move from a self-seeking life and ministry to a more community-based life and ministry.

CONTINUING EDUCATION

Open Enrollment

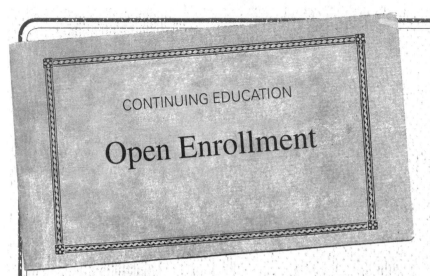

Open Enrollment

Soul Lesson: Soul School offers an open-enrollment education that lasts a lifetime. Classes are ongoing...

So many of us have stumbled into the crazy land of youth ministry and then found ourselves wondering from time to time: "What am I doing here?" For some of you, the journey began because someone believed in you as you were walking through your adolescent years, and it made all the difference in your world—so you've devoted yourself to trying to offer that gift to others. Or perhaps you journeyed through that fundamental life-shaping season feeling alone and insignificant, desperately wanting some adult to notice you and help shape a dream for your life, so you decided to try to be that person for someone else in the next generation. Maybe you looked at all the different areas of the church where you might get involved and found yourself drawn to youth ministry because it sounded a lot more exciting than counting the offering or directing traffic on Sunday mornings. And many of you felt such a clear and direct call from God into this work that you are now loving and leading students because you know there's no other place God would want you to be. Whatever your path into the crazy and sometimes unpredictable land of youth ministry, my hope is that you'll know the redemptive potential that awaits when God uses you to instill vision, hope, and belief into the life of a student.

If you've spent much time at all as a resident of the youth ministry world, you've probably realized it's a lot harder than it looks. Students don't always listen, they don't always appreciate or thank you, and sometimes they even make fun of you. Parents are often disappointed and difficult to please. You've probably felt the pressure at times to have more fun—or to be more serious. Perhaps you've messed up and then had to walk away from students who were just starting to offer their trust. And you've probably known the pain of watching students you love make poor choices and walk away from the church and from God.

The challenges of youth ministry are many and varied. Most every youth worker has felt the pressure to perform for a supervisor and attract more students to the ministry. Most of us know how it feels to lead a disappointing small group or to look into the blank faces of students while delivering our message, as if we were speaking another language. If you've been a youth pastor long, you've probably prayed prayers that God seems to have left unanswered. Perhaps you've wondered why you weren't doing something that seemed more "important" to others. You've struggled with motives, made mistakes, and compared your ministry to the larger ministry down the street. You've probably even wanted to quit. And on top of all these struggles, you've probably found that being part of the youth ministry has brought the deeper things in your soul to the surface. Youth ministry is hard, and it cannot be done without learning to live from your soul.

> The possibility of transformation is the essence of hope.
>
> JOHN ORTBERG

If you've made it this far in the book, then you've probably realized that enrolling in the School of the Soul is the only real chance you have to stay "alive" in youth ministry. You probably also recognize that Soul School is not a 3-credit required course that you can complete in a couple of months. It is an open enrollment program that is to be taken for the rest of our lives. We need to continually tune up our souls and engage in the life principles discussed in *Soul School*. And we need to invite others on the journey and mentor them in the ways of the soul.

The world is begging for authentic individuals with a strong core and a committed spirit. The ongoing School of the Soul is looking for people who are willing to commit to this maturing process. But it's a process that takes time—part of the Soul School curriculum is learning to wait. We must also be willing to engage with the pain we encounter. There have been many times when I've walked through an uncomfortable maturing experience eager to get to the other side. But if I do not rush the journey, I find that God often ushers me into yet another layer of continuing to mature my soul for the sake of transformation. The joy of this journey is that transformation never ends—but it requires great patience and trust along the way.

TAKING THE LONG WAY ROUND

I hate getting lost—and I hate being late even more. That sense of having no idea where I am and knowing I was supposed to be somewhere five minutes ago is a terrible tension for me. When I first discovered MapQuest a few years ago, I thought I might never have to feel that way again. But there have been too many moments when even those precise computer-generated directions have sent me down the wrong path. So when my husband and I bought a "new" used car that had a navigation system installed, I was hopeful that I'd increase my odds of remaining on course and on time.

The satellite technology is amazing, and so far it has not let me down. Somehow it knows exactly where I am at all times. When I type in the address for my destination, it often gives me 3 different options for getting there: the fastest route, the route without highways, and the scenic route. So far I've only used the first two options. As someone who is quite impatient and often in a hurry, I've never been inclined to take the extra time that the more scenic route requires.

My spiritual life is not much different. My dislike of getting lost and being late has an uncanny resemblance to my feelings around spiritual waiting. Transformation is something I desire, but I've often struggled with the route God chooses to get me there. I've often wondered if God feels like he's playing a broken record with me, because he has had to use the word *wait* so often in my life.

Sue Monk Kidd stresses the spiritual value of learning to wait. She writes:

> Transformations come only as we go the long way round, only as we're
> willing to walk a different, longer, more arduous, more inward, more
> prayerful route. When you wait, you're deliberately choosing to take the

long way, to go eight blocks instead of four, trusting that there's a transforming discovery lying pooled along the way.

As an enrolled student of Soul School, I've found the maturing course on waiting to be one of the hardest subjects. Every time I think I've made a little headway in this course, I find myself failing some small pop quiz. Sometimes it's as simple as having to wait in a long line at the supermarket; other times it's a more serious assignment, like waiting for God to reveal why he has me in a certain place when all I want to do is give up and leave. Spiritual waiting is frustrating for many of us; it can cause us to wonder if God will ever operate within the time frame we desire. But the Scriptures are packed with God's kind but firm voice telling his people to wait. He knows that in the process of waiting we learn to trust him at a much deeper level.

I've learned over time that great contentment comes when we remain in the posture of waiting. Somehow when we wait, we begin to inhale the peace of God and exhale the lives we were intended to live. Even though I'm not usually the one to choose to take the eight-block route instead of the four, every time God has placed me on a "long way round" path, he has been faithful to deepen my character and mature my trust. He has reminded me that he is faithful and present, even when I'm on the scenic route.

Perhaps there's a prayer you've prayed for a long time, and you're tired of waiting on God's answer. Maybe you desire something good and right that God has not given to you—and you are tired of being hopeful. Maybe you've long hoped for a change that hasn't occurred, and you feel like giving up and walking away. Remember that God may have you waiting right now to mature you. God may be directing you down the scenic route in order to transform you so you are more like Jesus.

So how are you at waiting? If you're like me and you need to take this particular class again and again, take heart as you continue to wait. Your soul depends on it.

WOUNDS: GOD'S MEGAPHONE

C.S. Lewis once wrote, "God whispers to us in our pleasures, speaks in our conscious, but shouts in our pains: It is his megaphone to rouse a deaf world." Pain can sound a loud spiritual alarm in a person's life. When the dark unthinkable moments happen, we cry out to be rescued from our tribulations and trials. But the path of pain is unavoidable if we truly desire transformation. It is in the darkness and discomfort of the cocoon that God begins to draw us toward wholeness. Many of us are afraid that we will never recover from the deepest wounds we experience, but it is by traveling through the passage from pain to possibility that we begin to move toward a reconciled wholeness and healed heart.

It was an unusually warm Sunday morning in September. Our student ministry team wanted to make sure it was a special morning since it was the first Sunday of the new school year. We'd done a bit of a makeover of our student ministry room over the summer so we were excited for students and leaders to see the final result. Although my husband, Jarrett, usually has other church responsibilities he needs to handle on Sunday mornings, this day was an exception, and he came to the student ministry with me.

I was in the middle of my message when someone's cell phone rang. I didn't make a big deal about it and continued with my talk. That day, I was showing a video clip to the students as part of my message. So I set up the video clip and sat down on the front row. The second I sat down, my husband grabbed my arm and told me I needed to pick up all my things and come with him. I told him I still needed to finish my talk—but he insisted that everything would be taken care of and I needed to leave. His eyes were convincing, so I quietly gathered my things and walked out. As we got into the hallway I asked him what was wrong. He said, "I'll tell you in a moment." I panicked and demanded that he tell me what was going on. So as we descended the staircase, Jarrett explained that he'd received a call from my brother during the service. My dad

> One of the most wonderful gifts we receive from a soul friend is that of a new perspective. He or she is able to stir up our imagination so that we not only view the past differently, but also allow the future to be filled with new, exciting possibilities.
>
> —ALAN JONES

had collapsed while running in a race with my youngest brother that morning, and they did not think he would make it. I froze. My mind couldn't process what he said. He wrapped his arms around me and walked me to our car as he repeated the news about my dad.

I have little memory of the car ride from the church to the hospital where my dad was taken. I know there was screaming and crying and pleading with God that it would not be true. The wound that was ripping through my heart was debilitating and devastating. My brothers met me at the hospital entrance and greeted me with the news that Dad did not receive the proper medical attention in time, and they were unable to save him. I disintegrated in their arms with grief and pain like I had never tasted. In a split second without any warning, my young and healthy father was gone. My mom, who had been married to my dad for 35 years, was suddenly a widow. My brothers and I were now children with only one parent. My husband and sister-in-law lost their father-in-law, and the children I'd have one day would never meet their grandfather. Coworkers lost a colleague. Other family members lost a brother or an uncle. Many, many others lost a friend.

My dad was coach, friend, father, cheerleader, supporter, caregiver, and provider. He understood me and knew how to love me well. Losing him drove me to a place of pain I'd never been to before. I did not want to live in the depth of loss I was experiencing; I just wanted my dad back. Well-meaning people offered words they hoped would bring peace and comfort, but I felt unsure the wound would ever really heal.

As painful as the loss of my father has been, God has used this journey more than any other experience in my life to bring about transformation in my life. I am not the same person I was. I pray differently. I speak to people differently. I cherish relationships differently. I value life differently. I bless others differently. The depth of pain and loss changed me from the inside out. I still miss my dad everyday, but the pain from his loss has changed who I am.

Pain will change you. It will transform you... if you let it. Whether the pain be from a wound inflicted on you by someone else, a wound you caused another person, or even the wounds that you have no control over—every one of these is pregnant with possibility to mature you and cause you to live from the soul. I have come to realize that pain is one of the most certain things in this life. We all experience it. So how are you responding to the pain in your life?

WELCOMING SOULMATES

One of the saddest questions I've heard people in ministry pose to one another is, "Where can I find a friend?" There is a temptation within the church to keep what lies beneath covered and hidden from community. But it is impossible to really live from your soul all by yourself. Our triune God dwells beautifully in relationship—Father, Son, and Spirit—and invites us to do the same. We are called to submit our whole selves—the good, the bad, and the ugly—to one another so that we can experience redemption and new formation together. Soul friendships are more than traveling companions on the road to new life; they are the image of the living God at work in his creation and a reminder of his constant loving presence. Soul friendships allow us to taste the goodness of being loved for who we really are, not what we've done.

I know far too many youth workers who are trying to walk through Soul School alone. When we drudge through class sitting alone in the corner, we miss some of the most valuable maturing growth that can happen in the School of the Soul. We need the views and perspectives of friends. Our pictures of our own lives are often jaded and one-sided. Soul friends can point us toward truth. They can confirm decisions. They can accompany us through the wonderful joys and great pains of life. My Soul School journey would be so different if I were not walking with others. The friends I've made along the way have kept me from dropping out of class when life gets hard and disappointing. Do you already have friends joining you on this journey of the soul? If not, I'd strongly encourage you to invite others to enroll with you.

CLASS IS ALWAYS IN SESSION

Society tells us that if we work hard and pay our dues, in time we'll be rewarded and we'll move on. Study hard in high school or college and one day you'll get that diploma that says that you've met all the requirements. But the School of the

Soul isn't like that. The journey through Soul School is ongoing, and asks that we return regularly to the same classes—mining them for deeper wisdom and greater truth. There's never a graduation ceremony where we throw our hats in the air and say good-bye to all we've learned and experienced.

Youth ministry requires leaders called and committed to being humble, faithful, and honest. Jesus told his disciples, "The greatest among you will be your servant. For those who exalt themselves will be humbled, and those who humble themselves will be exalted" (Matthew 23:11–12). It is only by committing ourselves in humility to this continuing journey that we can truly model the kind of leadership that will offer hope and life to our students.

When we are enrolled in Soul School, we allow love to be the center from which all ministry flows. We experience the grace that offers us true freedom and peace. We destroy the idols in our lives so that we can become authentic worshipers of the one true God.

In Soul School, we turn from our familiar roles as Performers, Pleasers, and Protectors so that we can instead live out our rightful calling as sons and daughters of God. We realize that becoming the true and unique people God created each of us to be is one of the greatest gifts any of us can offer our God and this world. We learn that by embracing what is broken within us, and by extending and receiving true forgiveness, we become miraculously whole and better able to reflect the love and beauty of Christ.

The School of the Soul reminds us that we must be healthy followers if we ever hope to be effective and influential leaders. We learn that our own selfish egos must be set aside if we would engage in healthy communal ministry. And we learn how to share the pen as together—with one another and with God—we cowrite the stories of our lives and ministry.

These soul lessons take a lifetime to learn. Soul School is an open enrollment education. Classes are ongoing; diplomas are never given.

The prayer I shared at the beginning of this book remains my desire for all those who read it. I pray that as you continue on this journey, you will find hope. I pray that you will enjoy the adventure of discovery—discovery of a true God and your true self. I pray that you'll open doors to parts of your soul that may have been locked for quite some time. I pray that you'll be gutsy enough to ask questions that can begin to illuminate the "whys" behind frivolous, busy activity. I pray that you will begin to name the destructive patterns in your life and ministry so that, with God's help, you can develop new and more life-giving ways. I pray that you'll develop a new blueprint for building emotional health and strength of the soul.

I pray that you'll enroll in a lifetime of study at the School of the Soul. I look forward to seeing you in class.

Contemplative Youth Ministry is a more organic approach to youth ministry, allowing you to create meaningful silence, foster covenant communities, engage students in contemplatice activities, and maximize spontaneity—and to help your students recognize the presence of Jesus in their everyday lives.

Contemplative Youth Ministry
Practicing the Presence of Jesus

Mark Yaconelli

RETAIL $21.99
ISBN 0-310-26777-3

youth specialties

Grounded in experience with real churches, this book chronicles the journey of more than a dozen youth ministries working to move Christian spirituality out of the retreat center and into the youth room. Youth pastors are growing tired of simply providing a ministry to distract and entertain teenagers. There is a growing desire for deeper, more authentic forms of adolescent discipleship. Grounded in experience with real churches, this book chronicles the journey of more than a dozen youth ministries working to move Christian spirituality out of the retreat center and into the youth room.

Growing Souls
Experiments in Contemplative Youth Ministry

Mark Yaconelli

RETAIL $21.99
ISBN 0-310-27328-5

youth
specialties